PRACTICAL GOURMET

Company's Coming®

400-Calorie
Slow Cooker

Paré • Billey

D1410722

Library and Archives Canada Cataloguing in Publication
Paré, Jean, author
        400-calorie slow cooker / Jean Paré.

(Original series)
Includes index.
ISBN 978-1-988133-04-1 (wire-o)

        1. Electric cooking, Slow. 2. Low-calorie diet--Recipes.
3. Cookbooks. I. Title. II. Title: Four hundred calorie slow
cooker. III. Series: Paré, Jean. Original series.

TX827.P3663 2016   641.5'884   C2015-906786-3

Distributed by
Canada Book Distributors - Booklogic
11414-119 Street
Edmonton. Alberta, Canada T5G 2X6
Tel: 1-800-661-9017

We acknowledge the financial support of the Government of Canada through the Canada Book Fund for our publishing activities.

Canadian   Patrimoine
Heritage   canadien

PC: 35

TABLE OF CONTENTS

The Jean Paré Story

Jean Paré (pronounced "jeen PAIR-ee") grew up understanding that the combination of family, friends and home cooking is the best recipe for a good life. When Jean left home, she took with her a love of cooking, many family recipes and an intriguing desire to read cookbooks as if they were novels!

When her four children had all reached school age, Jean volunteered to cater the 50th anniversary celebration of the Vermilion School of Agriculture, now Lakeland College, in Alberta, Canada. Working out of her home, Jean prepared a dinner for more than 1,000 people, launching a flourishing catering operation that continued for over 18 years.

"Never share a recipe you wouldn't use yourself."

As requests for her recipes increased, Jean was often asked the question, "Why don't you write a cookbook?" The publication of *150 Delicious Squares* on April 14, 1981 marked the debut of what would soon become one of the world's most popular cookbook series.

Company's Coming cookbooks are distributed in Canada, the United States, Australia and other world markets. Bestsellers many times over in English, Company's Coming cookbooks have also been published in French and Spanish.

Familiar and trusted in home kitchens around the world, Company's Coming cookbooks are offered in a variety of formats. Highly regarded as kitchen workbooks, the softcover Original Series, with its lay-flat plastic comb binding, is still a favourite among readers.

Jean Paré's approach to cooking has always called for quick and easy recipes using everyday ingredients. That view has served her well.

Jean continues to share what she calls The Golden Rule of Cooking: Never share a recipe you wouldn't use yourself. It's an approach that has worked—millions of times over!

Practical Gourmet

Good company and great food create a powerful combination. When laughter and conversation mix with the heady fragrance and flavours of delicious fare, we are not just sharing a meal—we are nourishing our lives. Artfully prepared dishes awaken the senses and please the palate. And here's the secret: It can all be so simple!

Company's Coming is delighted to introduce **Practical Gourmet**, a new series designed to help home cooks create no-fuss, sumptuous food. It is possible to wow both the eye and the palate using readily available ingredients and minimal effort. **Practical Gourmet** offers sophisticated recipes without the hassle of complicated methods, special equipment or obscure ingredients. Cook because you want to, the way you want to.

Each title features full-page colour photos of every recipe, preparation tips and tricks, and imaginative presentation ideas to allow you and your guests to savour the food…and your time together.

Introduction

For many people, maintaining (or achieving) a healthy weight can be a challenge. The market is flooded with specialty diets, weight-loss programs, foods, gadgets, apps, books, DVDs and the like, all geared to help the consumer reach or stay at their target weight. Some of these products may be helpful, others not as much, and a great deal of the information out there seems to be contradictory. But managing your weight doesn't need to be complicated. The bottom line is, to control your weight, you must control how many calories you eat.

Nutrition aside, it really doesn't matter how healthy the food is if you eat too much. Calories are calories, and whether they come from vegetables, meat or grains, they have the same function—to be burned as fuel for your body or reserved and stored as fat. For every 3500 calories you eat more than what your body burns, you gain 1 pound (454 g) of fat; if you burn 3500 more calories than you take in, you lose 1 pound (454 g) of fat. So the simplest way to manage your weight is to balance the number of calories you ingest with what your body burns.

Dietary guidelines in Canada and the U.S. indicate that adult men need between 2500 and 3000 calories per day, depending on their age and activity level. For women, the numbers are a bit lower, between 1900 and 2400 calories per day. Your height and weight also help determine where you fall in that range.

Watching your calories doesn't have to mean depriving yourself of the foods you love. The key is to make healthier food choices, watch portion sizes and practice moderation.

Fat contains more than twice as many calories as carbohydrates or protein (9 calories in 1 gram of fat vs. 4 calories in 1 gram of protein or carbs), and 1 Tbsp (15 mL) of fat has about 120 calories. For the same number of calories, you could eat 4 cups of broccoli or 17 cups of spinach (not that you'd want to, but you get the point.) To keep calories in check, limit the amount fat you use. Yes, fat is flavour, but broth, lemon juice, fresh herbs and spices can also add flavour with a lot less calories.

Protein and fibre keep you feeling full longer than simple carbohydrates, so try to work them into every meal. Lean meats and legumes are good sources of protein, and for fibre choose whole grains, vegetables and fruit.

Portion control definitely plays a role in calorie counting, but that doesn't mean you have to walk away from the table hungry. Portion sizes in North America have grown dramatically in the last few decades, and many of us eat far more calories than we realize. In this book, we keep the recipes under 400 calories, which leaves you enough room to add in a low-calorie side and leave the table satisfied. Use this pattern for your other meals in the day and you should still have enough calories left for a few healthy snacks, too.

Watching your calories doesn't have to be difficult, it just requires a little planning, which can be challenging in today's hectic world. Who has the time or energy to prepare a healthy, home-cooked meal when your meeting runs late, the kids have soccer practice, the dog needs walking and that project deadline is looming? Life just seems to get busier all the time, and for many of us, finding the time to cook a nutritious homemade meal seems an impossible task. It doesn't have to be.

The slow cooker is a busy cook's best friend. It does most of the work for you. The meals in *400-Calorie Slow Cooker* have been written specifically for a slow cooker and yield delicious results with little to no prep work. Turn the slow cooker on before you leave the house in the morning and come home to a healthy, nutritious home-cooked meal!

West Indies Beef

Whisk your taste buds away to the Caribbean with this exceptionally tender beef dish.

Paprika	1 tsp.	5 mL
Pepper	1/2 tsp.	2 mL
Inside round (or boneless blade) steak, trimmed of fat, cut into 3/4 inch (2 cm) cubes	2 lbs.	900 g
Cooking oil	2 tbsp.	30 mL
Chopped onion	1 1/2 cups	375 mL
Garlic cloves, minced (or 1/2 tsp., 2 mL, powder)	2	2
Chopped tomato	2 cups	500 mL
Chopped green pepper	1 cup	250 mL
Finely grated, peeled ginger root (or 1 tsp., 5 mL, ground ginger)	1 tbsp.	15 mL
Ground cumin	1/2 tsp.	2 mL
Cayenne pepper	1/4 tsp.	1 mL
Long-grain brown rice	1 cup	250 mL
Water	2 1/2 cups	625 mL
Salt	1 tsp.	5 mL

Combine first 6 ingredients in a medium bowl. Transfer to a 3 1/2 to 4 quart (3.5 to 4 L) slow cooker.

Stir in next 5 ingredients. Cook, covered, on Low for 7 to 8 hours, or on High for 3 to 4 hours.

Combine remaining 3 ingredients in a medium saucepan. Bring to a boil on medium. Reduce heat to medium-low. Simmer, covered, for 40 to 50 minutes, without stirring. Fluff rice with a fork. Serve with beef. Serves 6.

1 serving: 370 Calories; 9 g Total Fat (4 g Mono, 1.5 g Poly, 1.5 g Sat); 65 mg Cholesterol; 34 g Carbohydrate (4 g Fibre, 4 g Sugar); 38 g Protein; 95 mg Sodium

Steak Bake

A hearty medley of beef, potatoes, carrots and onions in a rich tomato sauce. For an extra splash of colour, add in some green beans.

Medium onion, sliced	1	1
Medium peeled potatoes, quartered	4	4
Medium carrots, sliced	4	4
Beef inside round (or blade) steak, cut into 1 inch (2.5 cm) pieces	2 lbs.	900 g
14 oz. (398 mL) can of diced tomatoes (with juice)	1	1
10 oz. (284 mL) can of low-sodium condensed tomato soup	1	1
Salt	1 tsp.	5 mL
Pepper	1/4 tsp.	1 mL
Garlic powder	1/4 tsp.	1 mL
Water	1/4 cup	60 mL
All-purpose flour	2 tbsp.	30 mL
Frozen cut green beans (optional)	2 cups	500 mL
Chopped green onion, for garnish		

Layer first 4 ingredients, in order given, in a 5 to 7 quart (5 to 7 L) slow cooker.

Combine next 5 ingredients in a medium bowl. Pour over steak. Cook, covered, on Low for 8 to 10 hours, or on High for 4 to 5 hours. Transfer steak to a plate using a slotted spoon. Cover to keep warm.

Stir water into flour in a small cup until smooth. Stir into mixture in slow cooker. Cook, covered, on High for 15 minutes until boiling and slightly thickened.

Add green beans, if using, and steak. Stir until heated through. Garnish with green onion. Serves 6.

1 serving: 370 Calories; 7 g Total Fat (3 g Mono, 0.5 g Poly, 2.5 g Sat); 65 mg Cholesterol; 38 g Carbohydrate (4 g Fibre, 7 g Sugar); 39 g Protein; 220 mg Sodium

Baked Meatballs in Wine

This dish has a subtle wine flavor with a pleasant blend of garlic and mushrooms.

Large eggs, fork-beaten	2	2
Fresh bread crumbs	3/4 cup	175 mL
Milk	1/3 cup	75 mL
Ground allspice	1/4 tsp.	1 mL
Salt	1 tsp.	5 mL
Pepper	1/8 tsp.	0.5 mL
Finely chopped onion	1/4 cup	60 mL
Extra-lean ground beef	2 lbs.	900 g
Cooking Oil	2 tsp.	10 mL
Small onion, finely chopped	1	1
Diced fresh mushrooms	1 cup	250 mL
Garlic cloves, minced (or 1/2 tsp., 2 mL, powder)	2	2
Butter (or hard margarine)	2 tbsp.	30 mL
All-purpose flour	2 tbsp.	30 mL
Prepared low-sodium beef broth	1 1/4 cup	300 mL
Dry (or alcohol-free) red wine	1/4 cup	60 mL

Chopped fresh parsley, for garnish

Combine first 8 ingredients in a large bowl. Mix well. Shape into 1 1/2 inch (3.8 cm) balls. Heat oil in a large frying pan on medium. Cook meatballs in batches until browned, about 3 to 5 minutes per batch. Arrange in a 4 to 5 quart (4 to 5 L) slow cooker.

Sauté onion, mushrooms and garlic in butter for 5 minutes until liquid from mushrooms is evaporated and onion is golden. Sprinkle with flour. Mix well. Slowly stir in broth and wine. Heat, stirring, until boiling and thickened. Pour sauce over meatballs. Cook, covered, on Low for 7 to 8 hours, or on High for 3 1/2 to 4 hours.

Garnish with parsley. Serves 8.

1 serving: *300 Calories; 15 g Total Fat (6 g Mono, 1 g Poly, 6 g Sat); 125 mg Cholesterol; 10 g Carbohydrate (trace Fibre, 2 g Sugar); 28 g Protein; 560 mg Sodium*

Mexican Beef Hash

This one-dish meal with Mexican flair makes a satisfying brunch or lunch for the whole family. To spice up this dish, replace the taco seasoning with 2 tsp. (10 mL) finely chopped chipotle peppers in adobo sauce and add a generous sprinkle of salt to the potato mixture.

Canola oil	2 tsp.	10 mL
Extra-lean ground beef	1 lb.	454 g
Diced cooked potato	4 cups	1 L
Chili powder	1 tsp.	5 mL
Paprika	1/2 tsp.	2 mL
Ground cumin	1/2 tsp.	2 mL
Pepper	1/2 tsp.	2 mL
Salt	1/4 tsp.	1 mL
Garlic powder	1/2 tsp.	2 mL
Onion powder	1/4 tsp.	1 mL
Red pepper flakes	1/2 tsp.	2 mL
Dried oregano	1/4 tsp.	1 mL
Large eggs	6	6
Chopped, seeded tomato	1 cup	250 mL
Chopped onion	2 cups	500 mL
10 oz. (285 g) can of low-sodium condensed cheddar cheese (or cream of onion) soup	1	1

Heat canola oil in a large frying pan on medium-high. Scramble-fry ground beef for about 5 minutes until no longer pink. Transfer to a large bowl.

Add next 10 ingredients. Stir well. Transfer to well-greased 3 1/2 to 4 quart (3.5 to 4 L) slow cooker.

Whisk eggs, tomatoes, onion and soup in a medium bowl until smooth. Stir into beef mixture. Cook, covered, on High for about 2 hours until set. Serves 6.

1 serving: 400 Calories; 20 g Total Fat (8 g Mono, 2 g Poly, 8 g Sat); 55 mg Cholesterol; 31 g Carbohydrate (3 g Fibre, 5 g Sugar); 26 g Protein; 420 mg Sodium

Onion Pepper Swiss Steak

Serve up steak with tangy tomatoes for a weekend supper for the family. Pairs well with garlic mashed potatoes or rice.

Boneless beef blade steaks, trimmed of fat, cut into 4 pieces	1 1/2 lbs.	680 g
Salt, to taste		
Pepper, to taste		
All-purpose flour	3 tbsp.	45 mL
14 oz. (398 mL) can of whole tomatoes (with juice)	1	1
Chopped onion	2 cups	500 mL
Chopped red or green pepper	1 3/4 cups	425 mL
Garlic cloves, minced	2	2
Salt, to taste		
Pepper, to taste		
Chopped fresh thyme	2 tbsp.	30 mL

Sprinkle steaks with salt and pepper. Press into flour in a small, shallow dish until coated on all sides. Heat large greased frying pan on medium-high. Add steaks. Cook for about 2 minutes per side until browned. Transfer to a 3 1/2 to 4 quart (3.5 to 4 L) slow cooker.

Crush tomatoes by hand and add to slow cooker. Stir in next 5 ingredients. Cook, covered, on Low for 6 to 7 hours, or on High for 3 to 3 1/2 hours. Transfer to a serving platter. Sprinkle with chopped thyme. Serves 4.

1 serving: 340 Calories; 12 g Total Fat (5 g Mono, 0.5 g Poly, 4.5 g Sat); 90 mg Cholesterol; 19 g Carbohydrate (3 g Fibre, 7 g Sugar); 35 g Protein; 350 mg Sodium

Beef and Tomato Paprikash

Tender, bite-sized beef pairs well with tomatoes and paprika in this rich, saucy dish. It can be served with boiled potatoes or spooned over egg noodles.

Chopped onion	1 1/2 cups	375 mL
Boneless beef blade steak, trimmed of fat, cut into 1 inch (2.5 cm) cubes	2 1/2 lbs.	1.1 kg
Salt, to taste		
Pepper, to taste		
14 oz. (398 mL) can of diced tomatoes (with juice)	1	1
5 1/2 oz. (156 mL) can of tomato paste (see Tip, below)	1	1
Chopped red pepper	2 cups	500 mL
Caraway seeds	1 tbsp.	15 mL
Garlic cloves, minced	2	2
Paprika	2 tbsp.	30 mL
Water	1/2 cup	125 mL
Light sour cream	1 cup	250 mL
Chopped fresh oregano	1 tbsp.	15 mL

Put onion in a 4 to 5 quart (4 to 5 L) slow cooker. Arrange beef over top. Sprinkle with salt and pepper.

Combine next 7 ingredients in a medium bowl. Pour over beef. Cook, covered, on Low for 8 to 10 hours, or on High for 4 to 5 hours.

Stir in last two ingredients and cook, covered, on High for 10 minutes. Serves 6.

1 serving: 400 Calories; 19 g Total Fat (7 g Mono, 1 g Poly, 8 g Sat); 105 mg Cholesterol; 19 g Carbohydrate (5 g Fibre, 9 g Sugar); 41 g Protein; 260 mg Sodium

Tip: If a recipe calls for less than an entire can of tomato paste, freeze the unopened can for 30 minutes. Open both ends and push the contents through one end. Slice off only what you need. Freeze the remaining paste in a resealable freezer bag or plastic wrap for future use.

Thai Red Curry Beef

This rich, mildly-spiced coconut curry features tender beef and baby potatoes.
Spoon some of the sauce over rice, or dunk in some naan.

Baby potatoes, cut in half	2 lbs.	900 g
Boneless beef round steak, trimmed of fat, cut into 1 inch (2.5 cm) cubes	2 lbs.	900 g
Salt, to taste		
Pepper, to taste		
Chopped sweet onion	2 cups	500 mL
Chopped red pepper	2 cups	500 mL
Chopped yellow pepper	2 cups	500 mL
Thai red curry paste	2 tbsp.	30 mL
Water	1 cup	250 mL
14 oz. (398 mL) can of coconut milk	1	1
Frozen green beans, cut	2 cups	500 mL
No-salt seasoning	1 tsp.	5 mL

Put potatoes into a 4 to 5 quart (4 to 5 L) slow cooker.

Heat a large, well-greased frying pan on medium-high. Cook beef, in 2 batches, for about 10 minutes per batch, stirring occasionally, until browned. Transfer to slow cooker. Sprinkle with salt and pepper.

Add onion and peppers to same greased frying pan. Reduce heat to medium. Cook for about 10 minutes, stirring occasionally, until starting to brown.

Add curry paste and water. Heat, stirring and scraping any brown bits from bottom of pan, until boiling. Pour over beef. Cook, covered, on Low for 8 to 9 hours, or on High for 4 to 4 1/2 hours.

Stir in coconut milk, green beans and no-salt seasoning. Cook, covered, on High for 15 minutes. Serves 8.

1 serving: 380 Calories; 16 g Total Fat (2.5 g Mono, 0 g Poly, 11 g Sat); 50 mg Cholesterol; 30 g Carbohydrate (3 g Fibre, 4 g Sugar); 31 g Protein; 220 mg Sodium

Chipotle Squash Chili

A healthy, flavourful version of hamburger casserole, made even better with the addition of fresh tomatoes, spinach and zucchini.

Canola oil	1 tbsp.	15 mL
Extra-lean ground beef	1 lb.	454 g
Chopped celery	1 cup	250 mL
Chopped onion	1 cup	250 mL
Diced carrot	1 cup	250 mL
Garlic cloves, minced (or 1/2 tsp., 2 mL, powder)	2	2
28 oz. (796 mL) can of diced tomatoes (with juice)	1	1
Chopped butternut squash	3 cups	750 mL
19 oz. (540 mL) can of black beans, rinsed and drained	1	1
14 oz. (398 mL) can of red kidney beans, rinsed and drained	1	1
Tomato paste (see Tip, page 18)	1/4 cup	60 mL
Dry (or alcohol-free) red wine	1/2 cup	125 mL
Chili powder	2 tbsp.	30 mL
Finely chopped chipotle peppers in adobo sauce (see Tip, page 44)	2 tsp.	10 mL
Pepper	1/4 tsp.	1 mL
Diced red pepper	1 cup	250 mL
Frozen kernel corn, thawed	1 cup	250 mL

Heat canola oil in a large frying pan on medium-high. Add beef. Scramble-fry for about 5 minutes until no longer pink.

Combine beef and next 13 ingredients in a 4 1/2 to 5 quart (4.5 to 5 L) slow cooker. Cook, covered, on Low for 7 to 8 hours, or on High for 3 1/2 to 4 hours.

Stir in red pepper and corn. Cook, covered, on High for 15 minutes. Serves 6.

1 serving: 380 Calories; 16 g Total Fat (2.5 g Mono, 0 g Poly, 11 g Sat); 50 mg Cholesterol; 30 g Carbohydrate (3 g Fibre, 4 g Sugar); 31 g Protein; 220 mg Sodium

Beef and Bean Casserole

A healthy, flavourful version of hamburger casserole, made even better with the addition of fresh tomatoes, spinach and zucchini.

Canola oil	1 tsp.	5 mL
Extra-lean ground beef	1/2 lb.	225 g
Chopped red onion	1 cup	250 mL
Garlic cloves, minced (or 1/2 tsp., 2 mL, powder)	2	2
Cooked orecchiette	3 cups	750 mL
Chopped tomato	2 cups	500 mL
Chopped fresh spinach leaves, lightly packed	1 1/2 cups	375 mL
Diced zucchini (with peel)	1 1/2 cups	375 mL
19 oz. (540 mL) can of mixed beans, rinsed and drained	1	1
7 1/2 oz. (213 mL) can of tomato sauce	1	1
Dry (or alcohol-free) red wine	1/2 cup	125 mL
Prepared low-sodium beef broth	1/2 cup	125 mL
Balsamic vinegar	1 tbsp.	15 mL
Italian seasoning	1 tsp.	5 mL
Pepper	1/4 tsp.	1 mL
Grated Parmesan cheese	1 cup	250 mL

Heat canola oil in a large frying pan on medium-high. Add next 3 ingredients. Scramble-fry for about 5 minutes until beef is no longer pink and onion is softened. Transfer to a 5 quart (5 L) slow cooker.

Stir next 11 ingredients into beef mixture. Cook, covered, on Low for 7 to 8 hours, or on High for 3 1/2 to 4 hours.

Sprinkle cheese over top and cook, covered, on High for 20 minutes. Serves 6.

1 serving: 390 Calories; 10 g Total Fat (3 g Mono, 1 g Poly, 4.5 g Sat); 35 mg Cholesterol; 46 g Carbohydrate (8 g Fibre, 5 g Sugar); 25 g Protein; 700 mg Sodium

Beef in Beer

Tender beef in a rich sauce tops thick French bread slices seasoned with Dijon mustard. For best results, use brown ale for its smooth, slightly sweet flavour.

Cooking oil	2 tsp.	10 mL
Chopped onion	1 cup	250 mL
Bacon slices, diced	4	4
All-purpose flour	2 tbsp	30 mL
Beef stew meat	2 lbs.	900 g
Cooking oil	1 tbsp.	15 mL
12 1/2 oz. (355 mL) can of beer	1	1
Dijon mustard	1 tbsp.	15 mL
Granulated sugar	2 tsp.	10 mL
Dried thyme	1 tsp.	5 mL
French bread slices (about 1 inch, 2.5 cm, thick), toasted	8	8
Dijon mustard	2 1/2 tbsp.	37 mL

Heat first amount of cooking oil in a large frying pan on medium. Add onion and bacon. Cook for 5 to 10 minutes, stirring often, until onion is softened. Transfer with a slotted spoon to a 3 1/2 to 4 quart (3.5 to 4 L) slow cooker. Discard drippings.

Measure flour into a large resealable freezer bag. Add 1/2 of beef. Seal bag and toss until beef is coated. Repeat with remaining beef. Heat second amount of cooking oil in same frying pan on medium. Add beef in 2 batches. Cook for 5 to 10 minutes per batch, stirring occasionally, until browned.

Combine next 4 ingredients in a 2 cup (500 mL) liquid measure. Slowly add to beef, stirring constantly and scraping any brown bits from bottom of pan, until boiling. Add to onion mixture. Stir well. Cook, covered, on Low for 8 to 9 hours, or on High for 4 to 4 1/2 hours.

Place 1 bread slice on each of 8 plates. Spread about 1 tsp. (5 mL) mustard on each bread slice. Spoon 1/2 cup (125 mL) beef mixture on top of each slice. Serves 8.

1 serving: 400 Calories; 18 g Total Fat (10 g Mono, 2 g Poly, 7 g Sat); 75 mg Cholesterol; 18 g Carbohydrate (trace Fibre, 2 g Sugar); 29 g Protein; 390 mg Sodium

Corned Beef Dinner

Tender corned beef and winter vegetables make a comforting meal. Strain and save the broth to use in your favourite soup recipe.

Baby carrots	1 lb.	454 g
Red baby potatoes, larger ones cut in half	1 lb.	454 g
Yellow medium turnip, cut into 1 inch (2.5 cm) cubes	1	1
Chopped onion	2 cups	500 mL
Corned beef brisket	2 lbs.	900 g
Water	4 cups	1 L
Bay leaves	2	2
Whole black peppercorns	1 tbsp.	15 mL

Layer first 4 ingredients, in order given, in a 5 to 7 quart (5 to 7 L) slow cooker. Place corned beef brisket on top, fat side up.

Add water, bay leaves and peppercorns. Do not stir. Cook, covered, on Low for 8 to 10 hours, or on High for 4 to 5 hours. Remove and discard bay leaves. Transfer corned beef to a large serving platter. Cut into thin slices. Transfer vegetables from slow cooker with a slotted spoon to a large serving bowl. Serve with corned beef. Serves 8.

1 serving: 260 Calories; 12 g Total Fat (5 g Mono, 0.5 g Poly, 3.5 g Sat); 60 mg Cholesterol; 21 g Carbohydrate (3 g Fibre, 5 g Sugar); 18 g Protein; 1190 mg Sodium

Rouladen

These tender beef and bacon rolls are bursting with smoky flavour for guest-worthy holiday fare. The mild, tasty gravy would be wonderful served over mashed or boiled potatoes.

Beef rouladen steaks, 1/4 inch (6 mm) thick	8	8
Prepared horseradish	3 tbsp.	45 mL
Pepper, to taste		
Bacon slices, cut in half	4	4
Thickly sliced red onion	1/4 cup	60 mL
Dill pickle, sliced lengthwise into 4 pieces	2	2
Wooden picks	8	8
1 1/2 oz. (42 g) envelope of onion soup mix	1	1
Minute tapioca	2 tbsp.	30 mL
Prepared low-sodium beef broth	1 1/2 cups	375 mL
Dry (or alcohol-free) red wine	1/2 cup	125 mL
Light sour cream	1/2 cup	125 mL

Arrange steaks on work surface. Spread about 1 tsp. (5 mL) horseradish over each steak. Sprinkle with pepper. Place 1/2 strip of bacon, some red onion and 1 strip of dill pickle on each steak. Starting at 1 short end, roll to enclose filling. Secure seam with a wooden pick. Arrange beef rolls, seam side down, in a single layer in a 4 to 5 quart (4 to 5 L) slow cooker.

Combine soup mix, tapioca, beef broth and red wine in a small bowl. Pour over beef. Do not stir. Cook, covered, on Low for 8 to 9 hours, or on High for 4 to 4 1/2 hours. Transfer rolls with a slotted spoon to a large serving platter. Cover to keep warm.

Skim and discard fat from cooking liquid. Add sour cream. Carefully process in a blender in batches until smooth, following manufacture's instructions for processing hot liquids. Pour sauce over rolls. Serves 8.

1 serving: 240 Calories; 14 g Total Fat (6 g Mono, 1 g Poly, 5 g Sat); 50 mg Cholesterol; 9 g Carbohydrate (trace Fibre, 2 g Sugar); 15 g Protein; 1000 mg Sodium

Goulash

Originating from a dish eaten by Hungarian shepherds as they braved the cold to watch their flocks, goulash has become a popular dish throughout much of Europe. A comforting mix of beef, tomato and paprika, this stew is the perfect meal for a cold winter day.

Chopped onion	2 cups	500 mL
Chopped red pepper	1 1/2 cups	375 mL
Garlic cloves, minced	2	2
All-purpose flour	2 tbsp.	30 mL
Hungarian paprika	1 tbsp.	15 mL
Salt	1 tsp.	5 mL
Pepper	1/2 tsp.	2 mL
Stewing beef, cut into 1 inch (2.5 cm) cubes	2 lbs.	900 g
14 oz. (398 mL) can of diced tomatoes (with juice)	1	1
Prepared low-sodium beef broth	1/2 cup	125 mL
Tomato paste (see Tip, page 18)	2 tsp.	10 mL
Bay leaves	2	2
Sugar	1 tsp.	5 mL
Light sour cream	1/2 cup	125 mL
Chopped fresh thyme	3 tbsp.	45 mL

Combine onion, red pepper and garlic in a 3 1/2 to 4 quart (3.5 to 4 L) slow cooker.

Combine next 4 ingredients in a large resealable freezer bag. Add beef, seal bag and toss until beef is coated. Add to slow cooker, discarding any remaining flour mixture.

Combine next 5 ingredients in a medium bowl. Stir into beef mixture in slow cooker. Cook, covered, on Low for 7 to 8 hours, or on High for 3 to 4 hours.

Remove bay leaves. Stir in sour cream and thyme. Serves 6.

1 serving: 340 Calories; 13 g Total Fat (4.5 g Mono, 1 g Poly, 5 g Sat); 80 mg Cholesterol; 17 g Carbohydrate (4 g Fibre, 7 g Sugar); 37 g Protein; 560 mg Sodium

Vietnamese Beef Stew

A slow cooker recipe with some Asian flair! Known as Bo Kho in Vietnamese, this stew pairs well with a loaf of fresh French bread or baguette.

Lemongrass stalks (4 inches, 10 cm long), cut and bruised	4	4
Fish sauce	1/4 cup	60 mL
Minced ginger root	2 tbsp.	30 mL
Brown sugar, packed	2 tsp.	10 mL
Chinese five-spice powder	1 1/2 tsp.	7 mL
Star anise, whole	2	2
Bay leaf	1	1
Stewing beef, cut into 1 inch (2.5 cm) pieces	2 lbs.	900 g
Canola oil	2 tsp.	10 mL
Chopped onion	2 cups	500 mL
Garlic clove, minced	2	2
Chopped carrot	2 cups	500 mL
Beef stock	2 cups	500 mL
28 oz. (796 mL) can of diced tomatoes	1	1
Cinnamon stick (3 to 4 inches, 7.5 to 10 cm, long)	2	2
Salt	1/2 tsp.	2 mL
Pepper	1/2 tsp.	2 mL
Chopped fresh cilantro	1/4 cup	60 mL

Combine first 7 ingredients in a resalable freezer bag. Add beef. Seal bag and let beef marinate in refrigerator for 1 hour, turning occasionally. Remove lemon grass, star anise and bay leaf from marinade and set aside.

Heat canola oil in a medium frying pan on medium. Remove beef from marinade and discard marinade. Cook beef, in two batches, for about 8 minutes per batch, stirring occasionally, until all sides are browned. Transfer with a slotted spoon to a 4 to 5 quart (4 to 5 L) slow cooker.

Add onions and garlic to same frying pan. Cook for about 5 minutes, stirring often, until onions start to soften. Transfer to slow cooker.

Stir in next 6 ingredients, reserved lemon grass, star anise and bay leaf. Cook, covered, on Low for 7 to 8 hours, or on High for 3 1/2 to 4 hours. Remove bay leaf, lemongrass, cinnamon stick and star anise. Stir in cilantro. Serves 4.

1 serving: 400 Calories; 15 g Total Fat (6 g Mono, 1 g Poly, 4.5 g Sat); 90 mg Cholesterol; 23 g Carbohydrate (3 g Fibre, 15 g Sugar); 44 g Protein; 850 mg Sodium

Thyme Beef Stew

Classic beef stew gets an added flavour boost with the addition of thyme and Dijon mustard.

Chopped carrots	3 cups	750 mL
Baby potatoes, larger ones cut in half	1 lb.	454 g
Chopped celery	1 1/4 cups	300 mL
Sliced onion	1 1/4 cups	300 mL
All-purpose flour	1/4 cup	60 mL
Paprika	1/4 tsp.	1 mL
Stew beef, cut into 1 inch (2.5 cm) pieces	1 1/2 lbs.	680 g
Cooking oil	2 tsp.	10 mL
Prepared low-sodium beef broth	1 ½ cups	375 m
Grainy Dijon mustard	1/3 cup	75 mL
Tomato paste (see Tip, page 18)	1 tbsp.	15 mL
Worcestershire sauce	2 tsp.	10 mL
No-salt seasoning	1 tsp.	5 mL
Pepper	1/2 tsp.	2 mL
Chopped red pepper	1 cup	250 mL
Chopped fresh thyme	2 tbsp.	30 mL
Chopped fresh parsley	1 tbsp.	15 mL

Combine first 4 ingredients in a 4 to 5 quart (4 to 5 L) slow cooker.

Combine flour and paprika in a large resalable freezer bag. Add beef, seal bag and toss until beef is coated.

Heat cooking oil in a large frying pan on medium. Add beef. Reserve remaining flour mixture. Cook beef for 7 to 10 minutes, stirring occasionally, until browned on all sides. Add to slow cooker.

Combine next 6 ingredients and remaining flour mixture in same frying pan. Heat, stirring, on medium until slightly thickened. Add to slow cooker. Stir. Cook, covered, on Low for 8 to 9 hours, or on High 4 to 4 1/2 hours.

Add red pepper, thyme and parsley. Stir cook covered on High for about 10 minutes until red pepper is tender crisp. Serves 6.

1 serving: 390 Calories; 11 g Total Fat (4 g Mono, 0.5 g Poly, 4 g Sat); 75 mg Cholesterol; 33 g Carbohydrate (4 g Fibre, 7 g Sugar); 38 g Protein; 560 mg Sodium

Caribbean Curried Beef

Madras curry, lime and cilantro give this dish a bright, fresh flavour that really hits the spot when the weather is cool. Serve with rice or a warm roti.

Boneless beef blade roast, trimmed of fat and cut into 1 inch (2.5 cm) pieces	2 1/2 lbs.	1.1 kg
Medium potatoes, peeled and cut into 1 inch (2.5 cm) pieces	3	3
Sliced onion	1 cup	250 mL
Sliced green onions	1/4 cup	60 mL
Garlic cloves, minced	3	3
Madras curry powder	3 tbsp.	45 mL
Vegetable oil	2 tbsp.	30 mL
Chopped cilantro	2 tbsp.	30 mL
Chopped marjoram	1 tbsp.	15 mL
Caribbean no-salt seasoning	1 tsp.	5 mL
Pepper	1/2 tsp.	2 mL
Prepared low-sodium beef broth	1 cup	250 mL
Beer	1/2 cup	125 mL
All-purpose flour	2 tbsp.	30 mL
Prepared low-sodium beef broth	3 tbsp.	45 m
Lime juice	1 tbsp.	15 mL
Chopped fresh cilantro	1 tbsp.	15 mL

Combine first 11 ingredients in a 4 to 5 quart (4 to 5 L) slow cooker. Stir in broth and beer. Cook, covered, on Low for 7 to 8 hours, or on High for 3 1/2 to 4 hours.

Whisk flour with second amount of beef broth until smooth. Whisk mixture into slow cooker. Cook, covered, on High for about 10 minutes until slightly thickened.

Stir in lime juice and cilantro. Serves 6.

1 serving: 380 Calories; 14 g Total Fat (7 g Mono, 1.5 g Poly, 3.5 g Sat); 80 mg Cholesterol; 27 g Carbohydrate (4 g Fibre, 2 g Sugar); 33 g Protein; 250 mg Sodium

Greek Beef and Bean Medley

A comforting bean and beef dish with the zing of lemon, marinated artichokes and sharp feta.

19 oz. (540 mL) cans of chickpeas, drained and rinsed	2	2
19 oz. (540 mL) cans of romano beans drained and rinsed	2	2
14 oz. (398 mL) can of crushed tomatoes	1	1
14 oz. (398 mL) can of diced tomatoes	1	1
Diced carrot	1 cup	250 mL
Diced fennel	1 cup	250 mL
Diced turnip	1 cup	250 mL
Dry (or alcohol-free) red wine	3/4 cup	175 mL
Balsamic vinegar	2 tbsp.	30 mL
No-salt herb and garlic seasoning	1 tbsp.	15 mL
Garlic cloves, minced	3	3
Pepper	1/4 tsp.	1 mL
Boneless beef blade steak roast, trimmed of fat and cut into 1 inch (2.5 cm) pieces	1 1/2 lbs.	680 g
Grated lemon zest	1 tsp.	5 mL
Chopped spinach	2 cup	500 mL
6 oz. (170 mL) jar of marinated artichokes, drained and chopped	1	1
Chopped tomato	1/3 cup	75 mL
Crumbled feta cheese	1/3 cup	75 mL
Chopped fresh oregano	1 tbsp.	15 mL

Combine first 13 ingredients in a 4 to 5 quart (4 to 5 L) slow cooker. Cook, covered, on Low for 6 to 8 hours, or on High for 3 to 4 hours.

Stir in lemon zest and spinach. Cook, covered, on High for 20 minutes. Transfer to a serving bowl.

Scatter remaining 4 ingredients over top. Serves 8.

1 serving: 400 Calories; 18 g Total Fat (7 g Mono, 0.5 g Poly, 7 g Sat); 65 mg Cholesterol; 33 g Carbohydrate (10 g Fibre, 6 g Sugar); 25 g Protein; 530 mg Sodium

Braised Short Ribs

Definitely not short on flavour, these ribs have a sweet, tangy sauce and are so tender they practically fall off the bone. Serve with mashed potatoes.

All-purpose flour	1/4 cup	60 mL
Brown sugar, packed	2 tbsp.	30 mL
Ground cumin	1 tsp.	5 mL
Ground cinnamon	1/2 tsp.	2 mL
Dried thyme	1/2 tsp.	2 mL
Garlic cloves, minced	2	2
No-salt seasoning	1/2 tsp.	2 mL
Pepper	1/2 tsp.	2 mL
Beef short ribs, bone in, trimmed of fat	2 1/2 lbs.	1.1 kg
Diced red onion	2 cups	500 mL
Diced carrot	1 cup	250 mL
Diced celery	1/2 cup	125 mL
Garlic cloves, minced	4	4
Dry (or alcohol-free) red wine	1 cup	250 mL
Prepared low-sodium beef broth	6 cups	1.5 L
Rice wine vinegar	3/4 cup	175 mL
Sugar	3 tbsp.	45 mL
Fresh thyme sprigs	3	3
Cardamom pods, bruised	2	2
Star anise	2	2
Cinnamon stick	1	1
Bay leaf	2	2
Chopped green onions	1/3 cup	75 mL

Combine first 8 ingredients in a small bowl. Sprinkle over ribs and rub into meat. If there is any spice rub left, set aside. Arrange meat in a single layer in a 6 to 7 quart (6 to 7 L) slow cooker.

Arrange onions, carrots, celery and garlic around ribs.

Combine next 9 ingredients in a medium bowl. Pour over ribs. Cook, covered, on Low for 8 to 9 hours, or on High for 4 to 4 1/2 hours.

Remove ribs to a serving plate and cover to keep warm. Remove thyme, cardamom pods, star anise, cinnamon stick and bay leaves. Skim off any fat from sauce. Add any remaining spice mixture to liquid. Purée liquid using a hand blender. Return ribs to slow cooker, turning meat to coat. Garnish with green onions. Serves 6.

1 serving: 400 Calories; 16 g Total Fat (7 g Mono, 0 g Poly, 7 g Sat); 75 mg Cholesterol; 30 g Carbohydrate (2 g Fibre, 20 g Sugar); 29 g Protein; 780 mg Sodium

Pork with Orange Sauce

Apricot, Dijon, orange juice and a touch of brandy make this pork dish a meal you won't soon forget!

Apricot jam, warmed	1/4 cup	60 mL
Dijon mustard (with whole seeds)	2 tbsp.	30 mL
Salt, sprinkle		
Pepper, sprinkle		
Pork sirloin (or boneless loin) roast	3 lbs.	1.4 kg
Butter (or hard margarine)	1 tsp.	5 mL
Finely chopped onion	1/4 cup	60 mL
Brandy (or 2 tsp., 10 mL, brandy extract)	1/4 cup	60 mL
Orange juice	1 cup	250 mL
Prepared low-sodium chicken broth	1 cup	250 mL
Orange marmalade	1/2 cup	125 mL
Dijon mustard (with whole seeds)	1 tbsp.	15 mL
Water	1 tbsp.	15 mL
Cornstarch	2 tsp.	10 mL

Combine first 4 ingredients in a small cup. Brush over roast. Place roast in a 4 to 5 quart (4 to 5 L) slow cooker. Cook, covered, on Low for 8 hours, or on High for 4 hours. Transfer to a cutting board. Cover with foil and let stand for 10 minutes.

For the sauce, melt margarine in a medium saucepan on medium. Add onion. Cook for 5 to 10 minutes, stirring often, until softened and starting to brown.

Add brandy. Heat, stirring, for about 2 minutes until liquid is almost evaporated.

Stir in next 4 ingredients. Bring to a boil on medium-high. Boil, uncovered, for about 5 minutes until slightly reduced. Reduce heat to medium.

Stir water into cornstarch in a small cup. Add to orange juice mixture. Heat, stirring, for about 5 minutes until boiling and thickened. Cut roast into thin slices and serve with sauce. Serves 8.

1 serving: 350 Calories; 7 g Total Fat (3 g Mono, 0.5 g Poly, 2.5 g Sat); 100 mg Cholesterol; 2.5 g Carbohydrate (0 g Fibre, 19 g Sugar); 39 g Protein; 270 mg Sodium

Irish Stew

There's an extra touch of "Irish" in this simple lamb and vegetable stew—dark stout beer, such as Ireland's famous Guinness, is simmered in the broth. You can substitute a honey brown or a lager beer if you want a lighter tasting broth.

Baby potatoes, larger ones cut in half	1 lb.	454 g
Chopped carrots	2 cups	500 mL
Garlic cloves, minced	2	2
Cooking oil	2 tsp.	10 mL
Boneless lamb shoulder, trimmed of fat and cut into 1 1/2 inch (3.8 cm) pieces	3 lbs.	1.4 kg
No-salt seasoning, to taste		
Pepper, to taste		
Stout beer	1 1/2 cups	375 mL
10 oz. (284 mL) can of condensed onion soup	1	1
Chopped parsely	2 tbsp.	30 mL

Combine potato, carrot and garlic in a 5 to 7 quart (5 to 7 L) slow cooker.

Sprinkle lamb with salt and pepper. Heat oil in a large frying pan on medium-high. Cook lamb, in 2 batches, for about 5 minutes per batch, stirring occasionally, until browned. Add to slow cooker.

Add beer and soup to same frying pan. Heat, stirring and scraping any brown bits from bottom of pan, until boiling. Stir into lamb mixture. Cook, covered, on Low for 8 to 10 hours, or on High for 4 to 5 hours. Sprinkle with parsely. Serves 7.

1 serving: 290 Calories; 9 g Total Fat (4 g Mono, 1 g Poly, 2.5 g Sat); 85 mg Cholesterol; 20 g Carbohydrate (2 g Fibre, 3 g Sugar); 29 g Protein; 490 mg Sodium

Coconut Rice and Pork

A blend of subtle coconut-infused rice with brightly coloured vegetables and pork. A complete meal that the whole family is sure to enjoy.

Cooking oil	2 tsp.	10 mL
Boneless fast-fry pork chops, cut into 1/2 inch (12 mm) slices	1 lb.	454 g
Chopped onion	1/3 cup	75 mL
Lemon pepper	1/2 tsp.	2 mL
Sliced carrot	2 cups	500 mL
14 oz. (398 mL) can of light coconut milk	1	1
Converted brown rice	1 cup	250 mL
Water	1/2 cup	125 mL
Grated lime zest	1 tsp.	5 mL
No-salt seasoning	1/2 tsp.	2 mL
Dried crushed chilies	1/4 tsp.	1 mL
Frozen cut green beans	2 cups	500 mL

Heat cooking oil in a large frying pan on medium-high. Add next 3 ingredients. Cook for about 3 minutes, stirring often, until pork is browned. Transfer to a 3 1/2 to 4 quart (3.5 to 4 L) slow cooker.

Stir in next 7 ingredients. Cook, covered, on Low for 6 to 7 hours, or on High for 3 to 3 1/2 hours.

Stir in beans. Cook on High for 20 to 25 minutes. Serves 6.

1 serving: 340 Calories; 15 g Total Fat (4.5 g Mono, 1.5 g Poly, 6 g Sat); 50 mg Cholesterol; 33 g Carbohydrate (4 g Fibre, 4 g Sugar); 19 g Protein; 250 mg Sodium

Fruity Lamb Tagine

Sweet lamb stew that's saucy enough to serve over couscous or brown basmati rice. Freeze leftovers in individual portions and reheat on the stovetop or in the microwave.

All-purpose flour	2 tbsp.	30 mL
Salt	1/4 tsp.	1 mL
Pepper	1/4 tsp.	1 mL
Boneless lamb shoulder, trimmed of fat and cut into 1 inch (2.5 cm) pieces	1 1/2 lbs.	680 g
Coarsely chopped onion	1 1/2 cups	375 mL
Ground coriander	1 tsp.	5 mL
Ground cumin	1 tsp.	5 mL
Garlic cloves, minced (or 1/2 tsp., 2 mL, powder)	2	2
Ground cinnamon	1/2 tsp.	2 mL
Cayenne pepper	1/8 tsp.	0.5 mL
14 oz. (398 mL) can of diced tomatoes (with juice)	1	1
Prepared chicken broth	1 1/4 cups	300 mL
Coarsely chopped dried apricot	1/2 cup	125 mL
Coarsely chopped pitted dates	1/2 cup	125 mL
Sliced natural almonds, toasted	1/4 cup	60 mL

Combine first 3 ingredients in large resealable freezer bag. Add lamb. Seal bag and toss until lamb is coated. Transfer lamb to a 3 1/2 to 4 quart (3.5 to 4 L) slow cooker.

Combine next 10 ingredients in a large bowl. Add to lamb and stir. Cook, covered, on Low for 7 to 8 hours, or on High for 3 ½ to 4 hours.

Scatter almonds over top. Serves 6.

1 serving: 280 Calories; 8 g Total Fat (3.5 g Mono, 1 g Poly, 2.5 g Sat); 75 mg Cholesterol; 28 g Carbohydrate (4 g Fibre, 18 g Sugar); 26 g Protein; 320 mg Sodium

Sweet and Sour Pork

Who needs Chinese take-out when you can create your own sweet and sour pork at home in your slow cooker? Serve over rice or noodles.

Lean pork, cubed	2 lbs.	900 g
Sliced green pepper	1 cup	250 mL
Sliced red pepper	1 cup	250 mL
Sliced carrot	1 cup	250 mL
14 oz. (398 mL) can of pinepple tidbits, drained	1	1
Brown sugar, packed	3/4 cup	175 mL
Water	1 cup	250 mL
White vinegar	1/2 cup	125 mL
Low-sodium soy sauce	1 tbsp.	15 mL
Water	1/3 cup	75 mL
Cornstarch	1/4 cup	60 mL
Sliced green onion	2 tbsp.	30 mL

Place first 5 ingredients in a 3 1/2 quart (3.5 L) slow cooker.

Combine brown sugar and first amount of water in a small bowl. Stir in vinegar and soy sauce. Pour over pork. Cook, covered, on Low for 8 to 10 hours, or on High for 4 to 5 hours. Tilt slow cooker and skim off any fat.

Stir second amount of water and cornstarch together in a small bowl. Add to slow cooker. Cook on High for 15 to 20 minutes to thicken sauce. Sprinkle green onion over top. Serves 6.

1 serving: 380 Calories; 8 g Total Fat (3.5 g Mono, 1 g Poly, 3 g Sat); 100 mg Cholesterol; 45 g Carbohydrate (2 g Fibre, 36 g Sugar); 32 g Protein; 200 mg Sodium

Jamaican Pork Couscous

Mildly spiced chops and a sweet couscous blend. Both components are made separately in the slow cooker—the couscous cooks up quickly and dinner is ready!

Brown sugar, packed	1 tsp.	5 mL
Dried thyme	1/2 tsp.	2 mL
Ground allspice	1/2 tsp.	2 mL
Ground ginger	1/2 tsp.	2 mL
Cayenne pepper	1/4 tsp.	1 mL
Ground cinnamon	1/4 tsp.	1 mL
Salt	1/4 tsp.	1 mL
Pepper	1/4 tsp.	1 mL
Bone-in pork chops (about 4 oz., 113 g., each), trimmed of fat	8	8
Canola oil	2 tsp.	10 mL
Chopped onion	1 1/2 cups	375 mL
Chopped peeled orange-fleshed sweet potato	1 1/2 cups	375 mL
Unsweetened applesauce	1 cup	250 mL
Prepared low-sodium chicken broth	3/4 cup	175 mL
Frozen peas, thawed	1 cup	250 mL
Whole wheat couscous	1 cup	250 mL
Lime juice	1 tbsp.	15 mL

Combine first 8 ingredients in a small cup. Rub over both sides of pork chops.

Heat canola oil in a large frying pan on medium-high. Cook pork chops, in 2 batches, for about 1 minute per side, until browned. Transfer to a large plate.

Combine next 4 ingredients in a 5 to 7 quart (5 to 7 L) slow cooker. Arrange pork chops over top. Do not stir. Place a double layer of tea towels over slow cooker liner. Cover with lid. Cook on Low for 5 to 6 hours, or on High for 2 1/2 to 3 hours. Transfer pork chops to a large serving plate. Cover to keep warm. Skim and discard fat from cooking liquid.

Stir remaining 3 ingredients into slow cooker. Cook, covered, on High for about 10 minutes until liquid is absorbed and couscous is tender. Serve with pork chops. Serves 8.

1 serving: 340 Calories; 14 g Total Fat (6 g Mono, 1.5 g Poly, 4.5 g Sat); 65 mg Cholesterol; 32 g Carbohydrate (4 g Fibre, 8 g Sugar); 24 g Protein; 230 mg Sodium

Autumn Pork and Apple Stew

A great stew for fall when temperatures are starting to cool. Serve over rice or mashed potatoes with a hearty crusty bread.

Baby carrots, halved	1 lb.	454 g
Vegetable cocktail juice (such as V8)	1 cup	250 mL
Small onions, quartered	2	2
No-salt seasoning	1 tsp.	5 mL
Dried whole oregano	1/2 tsp.	2 mL
Paprika	1/4 tsp.	1 mL
Pepper	1/4 tsp.	1 mL
Ground rosemary	1/8 tsp.	0.5 mL
Medium cooking apples (such as MacIntosh or Golden Delicious), peeled, cored and cut into 8 wedges each	2	2
Pork shoulder steak, trimmed of fat and cubed	2 lbs.	900 g
All-purpose flour	2 tbsp.	30 mL
Chopped fresh oregano	1 tbsp.	15 mL
Chopped fresh rosemary	2 tbsp.	30 mL
Vegetable cocktail juice (such as V8)	1/2 cup	125 mL
Chopped fresh rosemary	2 tbsp.	30 mL

Combine first 9 ingredients in a 4 to 5 quart (4 to 5 L) slow cooker. Arrange pork over mixture. Cook, covered, on Low for 6 to 7 hours, or on High for 3 to 3 1/2 hours.

Stir flour, herbs and second amount of juice in a small bowl until smooth. Stir into stew. Cook, covered, on High for 30 minutes. Sprinkle rosemary over top. Serves 6.

1 serving: 370 Calories; 18 g Total Fat (8 g Mono, 2 g Poly, 6 g Sat); 100 mg Cholesterol; 18 g Carbohydrate (3 g Fibre, 10 g Sugar); 33 g Protein; 300 mg Sodium

Chili Rhubarb Pork

This lean, moist pork roast has a sweet fruity sauce with a hint of spicy heat—just the thing to jazz up your next Sunday dinner.

Boneless pork loin roast	3 lbs.	1.4 kg
Salt, to taste		
Pepper, to taste		
Frozen rhubarb, thawed	1 cup	250 mL
Chopped onion	1 cup	250 mL
Prepared low-sodium beef broth	1 cup	250 mL
Ketchup	1/2 cup	125 mL
Brown sugar, packed	1/4 cup	60 mL
Chili paste (sambal oelek)	2 tsp.	10 mL
Ground cinnamon	1 tsp.	5 mL
Currants	1 1/2 cups	375 mL

Sprinkle roast with salt and pepper. Cook in a large greased frying pan on medium-high for about 8 minutes, turning occasionally, until browned on all sides. Transfer to a 4 to 5 quart (4 to 5 L) slow cooker.

Process next 7 ingredients in a blender or food processor until smooth. Add currants. Pour over roast. Cook, covered, on Low for 8 to 9 hours, or on High for 4 to 4 1/2 hours. Transfer roast to a cutting board. Cover with foil. Let stand for 10 minutes. Skim and discard fat from cooking liquid. Carefully process liquid in a blender until smooth, following manufacturer's instructions for processing hot liquids. Cut roast into thin slices and serve with sauce. Serves 10.

1 serving: *300 Calories; 7 g Total Fat (3.5 g Mono, 1 g Poly, 2.5 g Sat); 75 mg Cholesterol; 27 g Carbohydrate (2 g Fibre, 24 g Sugar); 31 g Protein; 300 mg Sodium*

French Lamb Casserole

This rich, comforting dish was inspired by the classic French cassoulet. Make it a meal with a fresh baguette, steamed green beans and a bottle of wine.

Lamb shank, trimmed of fat, meat cut into 3/4 inch (2 cm) pieces, bone reserved (see Note)	**1 lb.**	**454 g**
28 oz. (796 mL) can of diced tomatoes (with juice)	**1**	**1**
28 oz. (796 mL) can of black-eyed peas rinsed and drained	**1**	**1**
Smoked ham sausage, cut into 1/8 inch (3 mm) slices	**3 oz.**	**85 g**
Onion soup mix, stir before measuring	**3 tbsp.**	**45 mL**

Heat a medium greased frying pan on medium-high. Add lamb. Cook for about 8 minutes, stirring occasionally, until browned. Transfer to a 4 to 5 quart (4 to 5 L) slow cooker.

Stir in remaining 4 ingredients and add reserved bone. Cook, covered, on Low for 8 to 10 hours, or on High for 4 to 5 hours. Remove and discard bone. Serves 4.

Note: Lamb shanks are commonly found in frozen bulk packages. If using frozen shanks, remember to thaw them before using.

1 serving: 350 Calories; 8 g Total Fat (2.5 g Mono, 1 g Poly, 3 g Sat); 80 mg Cholesterol; 34 g Carbohydrate (8 g Fibre, 6 g Sugar); 36 g Protein; 640 mg Sodium

Pumpkin and Pork Curry

Enjoy a twist of curry heat with this thick and saucy pork and pumpkin stew. It is ideal for serving with brown basmati rice or whole wheat naan.

Pumpkin, peeled and diced	4 cups	1 L
Boneless pork shoulder, blade steak, trimmed of fat and cut into 1 inch (2.5 cm) pieces	2 lbs.	900 g
Canola oil	1 tsp.	5 mL
Chopped onion	1 cup	250 mL
Finely grated ginger root	1 tsp.	5 mL
Garlic clove, minced	2	2
Curry powder	2 tsp.	10 mL
Dried crushed chilies	1 tsp.	5 mL
Ground coriander	1 tsp.	5 mL
Ground cumin	1 tsp.	5 mL
Light coconut milk	1 cup	250 mL
Prepared low-sodium chicken broth	1 cup	250 mL
Tomato paste (see Tip, page 18)	2 tbsp.	30 mL
Whole green cardamom, bruised	6	6
Cinnamon stick	1	1
Salt	1/2 tsp.	2 mL
Chopped fresh cilantro	3 tbsp.	45 mL

Layer pumpkin and pork, in order given, in a 4 to 5 quart (4 to 5 L) slow cooker.

Heat canola oil in a medium frying pan on medium. Add next 3 ingredients. Cook for about 5 minutes, stirring often, until onion is softened.

Add next 4 ingredients. Heat, stirring, for about 1 minute until fragrant. Remove from heat.

Stir in next 6 ingredients. Add to slow cooker. Do not stir. Cook, covered, on Low for 8 to 9 hours, or on High for 4 to 4 1/2 hours. Remove and discard cardamom and cinnamon stick. Stir in cilantro. Serves 6.

1 serving: 380 Calories; 14 g Total Fat (5 g Mono, 1.5 g Poly, 6 g Sat); 95 mg Cholesterol; 11 g Carbohydrate (2 g Fibre, 4 g Sugar); 34 g Protein; 440 mg Sodium

Pulled Pork Sandwiches with Lemon Slaw

Think slow cookers are just for cold weather cooking? Think again! Cook up a batch of this delicious pulled pork for your next backyard barbecue.

Apple cider vinegar	1 cup	250 mL
Water	1 cup	250 mL
Worcestershire sauce	1/4 cup	60 mL
Ketchup	1/2 cup	125 mL
Lemon juice	1/4 cup	60 mL
Tomato paste (see Tip, page 18)	3 tbsp.	45 mL
Hot chili or pepper sauce (sriracha)	2 tbsp.	30 mL
Chili powder	1 1/2 tbsp.	22 mL
Garlic cloves, minced	6	6
Bay leaves	4	4
Brown sugar, packed	2 tbsp.	30 mL
Hot ground paprika	2 tsp.	10 mL
Garlic powder	1 tsp.	5 mL
Ground cumin	1 tsp.	5 mL
Chili powder	1/2 tsp.	2 mL
Boneless pork shoulder butt roast	2 1/2 lbs.	1.1 kg
Fresh lemon juice	1/3 cup	75 mL
Sugar	1 tsp.	5 mL
No-salt seasoning	3/4 tsp.	4 mL
Pepper	1/4 tsp.	1 mL
Olive oil	2 tbsp.	30 mL
Thinly sliced green cabbage	2 cups	500 mL
Thinly sliced red onion	1/2 cup	125 mL
Grated carrot	1/2 cup	125 mL
Whole wheat hamburger buns, toasted	8	8

For the barbecue sauce, combine first 10 ingredients in a small sauce pan. Bring to a boil. Reduce heat to medium-low. Simmer uncovered, for 15 minutes. Remove from heat and discard bay leaves. Set aside to cool.

Combine next 5 ingredients in a small bowl. Rub pork with spice mixture. Put roast into a 5 to 6 quart (5 to 6 L) slow cooker. Pour barbecue sauce over top of roast. Cook, covered, on Low for 6 to 8 hours, or High for 3 to

4 hours until tender. Transfer roast to a large plate or cutting board. Shred pork using 2 forks. Remove and discard any visible fat. Return pork to sauce.

For the slaw, combine next 4 ingredients in a large bowl, stirring with a whisk. Gradually add olive oil, whisking constantly. Add next 3 ingredients and toss well.

Place equal amounts of meat onto bottom half of each bun. Top with equal amounts of lemon slaw. Top with top halves of buns. Serves 8.

1 serving: 400 Calories; 14 g Total Fat (7 g Mono, 2 g Poly, 4 g Sat); 90 mg Cholesterol; 35 g Carbohydrate (5 g Fibre, 16 g Sugar); 35 g Protein; 700 mg Sodium

Peachy Dijon Pork Chops

Meaty chops slowly cooked in a summery peach mustard sauce. Serve over rice or noodles.

Brown sugar, packed	1 tbsp.	15 mL
Paprika	1 tbsp.	15 mL
Ground cumin	1 tsp.	5 mL
Onion powder	1 tsp.	5 mL
Garlic powder	1 tsp.	5 mL
Mustard powder	1 tsp.	5 mL
Salt	1/2 tsp.	2 mL
Pepper	1/2 tsp.	2 mL
Pork loin chops (about 4 oz., 113 g, each), trimmed of fat	6	6
Medium peaches, quartered, pit removed	3	3
Apple cider	1 cup	250 mL
Peach jam	1 cup	250 mL
Apple cider vinegar	1/2 cup	125 mL
Prepared low-sodium chicken stock	1/4 cup	60 mL
Garlic cloves, minced	5	5
Worcestershire sauce	2 tbsp.	30 mL
Dijon mustard	4 tsp.	20 mL
Red pepper flakes	1/2 tsp.	2 mL
No-salt seasoning	1/2 tsp.	2 mL
Pepper	1/4 tsp.	1 mL
All-purpose flour	2 tbsp.	30 mL
Diced peaches	1 cup	250 mL
Basil, chopped	3 tbsp.	45 mL
Olive oil	1 tbsp.	15 mL

Combine first 8 ingredients in a large baking dish. Add pork chops, turning to coat with spice rub. Cover and refrigerate for about 30 minutes.

Put peaches into a 4 to 5 quart (4 to 5 L) slow cooker. Arrange pork over peaches.

Combine next 10 ingredients in a bowl. Remove 1/2 cup (125 mL) liquid and pour remaining mixture over pork. Cook, covered, on Low for 7 to 8 hours, or on High for 3 1/2 to 4 hours.

Mix reserved liquid into flour and add to slow cooker. Cook, covered, on High for 20 minutes. Transfer pork and peaches to a serving platter. Carefully process liquid in slow cooker with a hand held blender until smooth.

For the salsa, combine last 3 ingredients together. Serve pork with sauce spooned overtop and salsa on the side. Serves 6.

1 serving: 380 Calories; 8 g Total Fat (4 g Mono, 1 g Poly, 2 g Sat); 60 mg Cholesterol; 54 g Carbohydrate (2 g Fibre, 43 g Sugar); 23 g Protein; 170 mg Sodium

Sage Fennel Pork Ragout

This ragout is loaded with nutritious spinach and has a pleasant Mediterranean flavour thanks to the fennel and sage—great for serving over pasta or rice.

Garlic cloves, minced	5	5
Olive oil	2 tsp.	10 mL
Dried marjoram	1 1/2 tsp.	7 mL
Ground dried sage	1 tsp.	5 mL
Salt	1/2 tsp.	5 mL
Pepper	1/2 tsp.	5 mL
Boneless pork shoulder blade steaks, trimmed of fat and cut into 1 inch (2.5 cm) cubes	2 1/2 lbs.	1.1 kg
Diced fennel	2 1/2 cups	625 mL
Diced carrot	1 1/2 cups	375 mL
Sliced onion	1 1 /2 cups	375 mL
14 oz. (398 mL) can of diced tomatoes, with juice	1	1
Bay leaves	2	2
Kalamata olives	1/2 cup	125 mL
Chopped fresh spinach leaves	2 cups	500 mL
Chopped fresh sage	1/4 cup	60 mL
Lemon zest	1 tsp.	5 mL

Combine first 6 ingredients in a medium bowl. Stir in pork and let marinate for 1 hour.

Combine next 6 ingredients in a 4 to 5 quart (4 to 5 L) slow cooker. Stir in pork mixture. Cook, covered, on Low for 7 to 8 hours, or on High for 3 1/2 to 4 hours.

Remove bay leaves. Stir in spinach, sage and lemon zest. Cook, covered, on High for 10 minutes. Serves 6.

1 serving: 370 Calories; 16 g Total Fat (7 g Mono, 1.5 g Poly, 4.5 g Sat); 110 mg Cholesterol; 14 g Carbohydrate (4 g Fibre, 3 g Sugar); 41 g Protein; 450 mg Sodium

Chorizo Stuffed Peppers

This hearty yet light meal has true Spanish flavours with chorizo, rice, tomatoes and Spanish paprika.

Large red peppers	**3**	**3**
Canola oil	2 tsp.	10 mL
Lean chorizo, casing removed, crumbled	3/4 lb.	340 g
Chopped onion	1 cup	250 mL
Garlic cloves, minced	2	2
Cooked brown rice (about 1/2 cup, 125 mL, uncooked)	1 1/2 cups	375 mL
Frozen kernel corn	1 cup	250 mL
14 oz. (398 mL) can of cannellini beans, rinsed and drained	1	1
14 oz., (398 mL) can of diced tomatoes,	1	1
Chopped Swiss chard leaves, stems removed	1/2 cup	125 mL
Smoked Spanish paprika	1 tsp.	5 mL
Orange zest	1 tsp.	5 mL
Salt	1/4 tsp.	1 mL
Pepper	1/4 tsp.	1 mL
Shredded reduced-fat Monterey Jack,	1/2 cup	125 mL
Water	1 1/2 cups	375 mL

Cut peppers in half lengthwise and remove seeds, stem and ribs.

Heat canola oil in a large frying pan on medium-high. Add chorizo. Scramble-fry for about 7 minutes until chorizo is no longer pink. Add next 2 ingredients and cook for 5 minutes, stirring often, until onion has softened. Remove from heat.

Stir in next 9 ingredients. Spoon into prepared peppers. Arrange, filling side up, in a 7 quart (7 L) slow cooker. Sprinkle each half with cheese.

Pour water around peppers. Cook, covered, on Low for 4 to 5 hours, or on High for 2 to 2 ½ hours. Serves 6.

1 serving: 400 Calories; 20 g Total Fat (0.5 g Mono, 0.5 g Poly, 8 g Sat); 50 mg Cholesterol; 35 g Carbohydrate (7 g Fibre, 8 g Sugar); 19 g Protein; 550 mg Sodium

Chipotle Chicken Loaf

By using convenient pre-shredded cheese, jarred salsa and bagged bread crumbs, this family-friendly meatloaf will give you more time to loaf around!

Large egg, fork-beaten	1	1
Finely chopped onion	1 1/2 cups	375 mL
Grated light Mexican cheese blend	1 cup	250 mL
Fine dry bread crumbs	1/2 cup	125 mL
Salsa	1/2 cup	125 mL
Garlic cloves, minced (or 1/2 tsp., 2 mL, powder)	2	2
Chili powder	1 tsp.	5 mL
Finely chopped chipotle pepper in adobo sauce (see Tip, below)	1 tsp.	5 mL
Salt	1/2 tsp.	2 mL
Pepper	1/4 tsp.	1 mL
Lean ground chicken	2 lbs.	900 g
Grated light Mexican cheese blend	1/2 cup	125 mL
Lime wedges, for garnish		

Combine first 10 ingredients in a large bowl.

Add chicken. Mix well. Press into greased 9 x 5 x 3 inch (22 x 12.5 x 7.5 cm) loaf pan. Place loaf pan in a 6 to 7 quart (6 to 7 L) slow cooker. Cook, covered, on Low for 7 to 8 hours, or on High for 3 1/2 to 4 hours.

Sprinkle second amount of cheese evenly over loaf. Cook, covered, on High for 20 minutes. Remove from slow cooker and let stand for 10 minutes. Cut into slices.

Garnish individual servings with lime wedges. Serves 8.

1 serving: 340 Calories; 20 g Total Fat (0 g Mono, 0 g Poly, 3 g Sat); 85 mg Cholesterol; 11 g Carbohydrate (trace Fibre, 3 g Sugar); 27 g Protein; 590 mg Sodium

Tip: Chipotle chili peppers in adobo sauce are smoked jalapeño peppers that are canned in a smoky red sauce. Adobo sauce is not as spicy as the chipotle pepper, but it still packs some heat. Be sure to wash your hands after handling. Store leftover chipotle chili peppers with sauce in airtight container in refrigerator for up to 1 year.

Festive Chicken

Enjoy the festive flavours of cranberry, orange, and cinnamon—any time of year! The sauce goes great with rice or noodles.

All-purpose flour	3 tbsp.	45 mL
Salt	1/4 tsp.	1 mL
Pepper	1/8 tsp.	0.5 mL
Paprika	1/8 tsp.	0.5 mL
Boneless, skinless chicken breasts (about 4 oz., 113 g, each)	6	6
Cooking oil	1 tbsp.	15 mL
Sliced carrots	2 cups	500 mL
Prepared chicken broth	1 cup	250 mL
Frozen (or fresh) cranberries	1 cup	250 mL
Dry (or alcohol-free) white wine	1/2 cup	125 mL
Frozen concentrated orange juice, thawed	1/3 cup	75 mL
Diced onion	1/4 cup	60 mL
Ground cinnamon	1/4 tsp.	1 mL
Ground ginger	1/4 tsp.	1 mL

Combine first 4 ingredients in a large resealable freezer bag. Add chicken, seal bag and toss until chicken is coated. Remove chicken. Reserve remaining flour mixture.

Heat cooking oil in a large frying pan on medium-high. Add chicken. Cook for 2 to 3 minutes per side until browned. Arrange in a 3 1/2 to 4 quart (3.5 to 4 L) slow cooker. Add carrot.

Stir broth into reserved flour mixture in a small bowl until smooth. Stir in remaining 6 ingredients. Pour over chicken. Cook, covered, on Low for 7 to 8 hours, or on High for 3 1/2 to 4 hours. Serves 6.

1 serving: 250 Calories; 4.5 g Total Fat (2 g Mono, 1 g Poly, 0.5 g Sat); 85 mg Cholesterol; 13 g Carbohydrate (1 g Fibre, 7 g Sugar); 36 g Protein; 310 mg Sodium

Chicken Paella

We've used saffron, though it's a tad pricey, to give this dish an authentic taste and look.

Cooking oil	1 tsp.	5 mL
Boneless, skinless chicken breasts (about 4 oz., 113 g, each), cut in 1 inch (2.5 cm) pieces	8	8
Chopped onion	1 cup	250 mL
Chopped red pepper	1 1/4 cups	300 mL
Jalapeño pepper, finely sliced	1	1
Garlic clove, minced (or 1/4 tsp., 1 mL, powder)	1	1
14 oz. (398 mL) can of diced tomatoes (with juice)	1	1
Dry (or alcohol-free) white wine	1/2 cup	125 mL
Dried rosemary	1 tsp.	5 mL
Paprika	1/2 tsp.	2 mL
Long-grain white rice	1 1/4 cups	300 mL
Saffron threads (or turmeric)	1/8 tsp.	0.5 mL
Prepared chicken broth	1 1/2 cups	375 mL
Frozen peas	2 cups	500 mL
14 oz. (398 mL) can of artichoke hearts, drained and quartered (optional)	1	1
Frozen, uncooked large shrimp (peeled and deveined), thawed (optional)	1/2 lb.	225 g

Heat cooking oil in a large frying pan on medium. Add chicken. Cook for 3 to 4 minutes per side until browned. Transfer to a 4 to 5 quart (4 to 5 L) slow cooker.

Stir in next 11 ingredients. Cook, covered, on Low for 5 to 6 hours, or on High for 2 1/2 to 3 hours.

Scatter remaining 3 ingredients over rice mixture. Cook, covered, on High for 20 minutes until artichokes and peas are heated through and shrimp are pink and curled. Serves 8.

1 serving: 300 Calories; 2.5 g Total Fat (1 g Mono, 0.5 g Poly, 0 g Sat); 65 mg Cholesterol; 31 g Carbohydrate (3 g Fibre, 5 g Sugar); 28 g Protein; 240 mg Sodium

Curious Chicken Chili

Chocolate and coffee might seem like unusual ingredients to add to chili, but they give this dish an incredible depth of flavour.

Cooking oil	2 tsp.	10 mL
Boneless, skinless chicken thighs, cut into 1/2 inch (12 mm) pieces	1 lb.	454 g
Chopped onions	1 1/2 cups	375 mL
Chopped green pepper	1 cup	250 mL
Diced jalapeño pepper	1 tbsp.	15 mL
Garlic cloves, minced (or 1/2 tsp., 2 mL, powder)	2	2
No-salt seasoning	1 tsp.	5 mL
14 oz. (398 mL) can of diced tomatoes (with juice)	1	1
14 oz. (398 mL) can of pineapple chunks (with juice)	1	1
14 oz. (398 mL) can of red kidney beans, rinsed and drained	1	1
Hot (or cold) strong prepared coffee	1 cup	250 mL
4 oz. (113 g) can of diced green chilies	1	1
Tomato paste (see Tip, page 18)	3 tbsp.	45 mL
Chili powder	2 tbsp.	30 mL
Semi-sweet chocolate baking square (1 oz., 28 g), grated	1	1
Ground cumin	1 tsp.	5 mL

Heat cooking oil in a large frying pan on medium-high. Add chicken. Cook for about 5 minutes, stirring often, until browned.

Add next 5 ingredients. Cook for about 5 minutes, stirring often, until onion starts to soften. Transfer to a 3 1/2 to 4 quart (3.5 to 4 L) slow cooker.

Stir in remaining 9 ingredients. Cook, covered, on Low for 4 hours, or on High for 2 hours. Serves 6.

1 serving: 270 Calories; 8 g Total Fat (2 g Mono, 1.5 g Poly, 2 g Sat); 65 mg Cholesterol; 32 g Carbohydrate (9 g Fibre, 16 g Sugar); 20 g Protein; 290 mg Sodium

Turkey Fricassee

As any fine French chef can tell you, fricassee is meat stewed in a white cream sauce. Add a little chopped carrot or red pepper if you'd like a shot of colour. Serve with rice.

Chopped celery	1 1/2 cups	375 mL
Chopped onion	2 cups	500 mL
Boneless, skinless turkey breast, cut into 3 inch (7.5 cm) pieces	1 lb.	454 g
Boneless, skinless turkey thighs, cut into 3 inch (7.5 cm) pieces	1 lb.	454 g
Sliced leek (white part only)	3 1/2 cups	875 mL
Butter (or hard margarine)	3 tbsp.	45 mL
Garlic cloves, minced (or 1/2 tsp., 2 mL, powder), optional	2	2
All-purpose flour	1/4 cup	60 mL
Prepared chicken broth	2 cups	500 mL
Dry (or alcohol-free) white wine	1/4 cup	60 mL
14 oz. (398 mL) can of artichoke hearts, drained and halved	1	1
Dried thyme	1 tsp.	5 mL
Seasoned salt	1 tsp.	5 mL
Pepper	1/4 tsp.	1 mL
5 1/2 oz. (160 mL) can of evaporated milk	1	1
Chopped chives	2 tbsp.	30 mL

Layer first 5 ingredients, in order given, in a 4 to 5 quart (4 to 5 L) slow cooker.

Melt butter in a medium saucepan on medium. Add garlic. Heat, stirring, for about 1 minute until fragrant. Add flour. Heat, stirring, for 1 minute.

Slowly add broth and wine, stirring constantly, until smooth. Heat, stirring, for about 7 minutes until boiling and thickened. Remove from heat.

Stir in next 4 ingredients. Pour over turkey mixture in slow cooker. Cook, covered, on Low for 8 to 9 hours, or on High for 4 to 4 1/2 hours.

Stir in evaporated milk and chives. Cook, covered, on High for about 15 minutes. Serves 8.

1 serving: 270 Calories; 8 g Total Fat (2.5 g Mono, 1 g Poly, 3.5 g Sat); 95 mg Cholesterol; 19 g Carbohydrate (4 g Fibre, 7 g Sugar); 29 g Protein; 460 mg Sodium

Turkey Rice Casserole

All your favourite festive flavours in one convenient casserole. Tender turkey,
sweet cranberries and nutty brown rice make a filling autumn meal.

Prepared low-sodium chicken broth	1 1/2 cups	375 mL
Chopped onion	1 cup	250 mL
Long-grain brown rice	1 cup	250 mL
Chopped celery	1/2 cup	125 mL
Dry (or alcohol-free) white wine	1/4 cup	60 mL
Dried sage	1/2 tsp.	2 mL
Dried thyme	1/2 tsp.	2 mL
Boneless, skinless turkey thighs, cut into 1 inch (2.5 cm) pieces	1 1/2 lbs.	680 g
No-salt seasoning	1/4 tsp.	1 mL
Pepper	1/4 tsp.	1 mL
Chopped dried cranberries	1/4 cup	60 mL
Chopped fresh parsley	2 tbsp.	30 mL

Combine first 7 ingredients in a 3 1/2 to 4 quart (3.5 to 4 L) slow cooker.

Sprinkle turkey with salt and pepper. Arrange over rice mixture. Cook, covered, on Low for 7 to 8 hours, or on High for 3 1/2 to 4 hours.

Sprinkle with cranberries and parsley. Serves 4.

1 serving: 320 Calories; 10 g Total Fat (4 g Mono, 1 g Poly, 3 g Sat); 15 mg Cholesterol; 49 g Carbohydrate (4 g Fibre, 8 g Sugar); 7 g Protein; 420 mg Sodium

Chicken Cacciatore

You won't miss Nonna's cacciatore once you've tasted this delicious version.
It goes well over pasta or rice.

Cooking oil	2 tsp.	10 mL
Chicken drumsticks, skin removed	1 1/2 lbs.	680 g
Chopped onion	1 cup	250 mL
Garlic cloves, minced (or 1/2 tsp., 2 mL, powder)	2	2
Dry (or alcohol-free) white wine	1/4 cup	60 mL
28 oz. (796 mL) can of diced tomatoes (with juice)	1	1
Chopped green pepper	2 cups	500 mL
Tomato paste (see Tip, page 18)	1/4 cup	60 mL
Bay leaf	1	1
Dried basil	1 tsp.	5 mL
Dried oregano	1 tsp.	5 mL
Granulated sugar	1 tsp.	5 mL
Dried rosemary, crushed	1/2 tsp.	2 mL
Salt	1/2 tsp.	2 mL
Pepper	1/4 tsp.	1 mL
Grated Parmesan cheese	1/2 cup	125 mL

Heat cooking oil in a large frying pan on medium-high. Add chicken. Cook, uncovered, for about 5 minutes, stirring occasionally, until chicken starts to brown.

Add next 2 ingredients. Cook for 5 to 10 minutes, stirring occasionally, until onion is softened.

Add wine. Heat, stirring, for 1 minute. Transfer to a 4 to 5 quart (4 to 5 L) slow cooker.

Stir in next 10 ingredients. Cook, covered, on Low for 6 to 7 hours, or on High for 3 to 3 1/2 hours.

Sprinkle with Parmesan cheese. Serves 6.

1 serving: *220 Calories; 9 g Total Fat (3 g Mono, 2 g Poly, 2.5 g Sat); 85 mg Cholesterol; 8 g Carbohydrate (1 g Fibre, 3 g Sugar); 24 g Protein; 410 mg Sodium*

Pineapple Chicken

This sweet and saucy chicken dish can be served over steamed rice.

Chicken breast, cut into 1 inch (2.5 cm) pieces	1 1/2 lbs.	680 g
19 oz. (540 mL) can of pineapple tidbits (with juice)	1	1
Chopped red pepper	2 cups	500 mL
Chopped celery	1 cup	250 mL
Chopped onion	1 cup	250 mL
Garlic clove, minced	2	2
Finely grated ginger root	1 tbsp.	15 mL
Prepared low-sodium chicken broth	1/2 cup	125 mL
Thick teriyaki basting sauce	1/2 cup	125 mL
Prepared low-sodium chicken broth	3 tbsp.	45 mL
Cornstarch	1 1/2 tbsp.	22 mL

Combine first 7 ingredients in a 3 1/2 to 4 quart (3.5 to 4 L) slow cooker.

Combine first amount of chicken broth and teriyaki sauce in a small bowl. Stir into chicken mixture. Cook, covered, on Low for 6 to 7 hours, or on High for 3 to 3 1/2 hours.

Stir second amount of chicken broth into cornstarch in a small cup until smooth. Stir into chicken mixture. Cook, covered, on High for about 10 minutes until sauce is slightly thickened. Serves 4.

1 serving: 350 Calories; 3 g Total Fat (0.5 g Mono, 1 g Poly, 1 g Sat); 100 mg Cholesterol; 38 g Carbohydrate (4 g Fibre, 30 g Sugar); 41 g Protein; 850 mg Sodium

Cajun Turkey Stew

Tender turkey and potatoes in a spicy tomato sauce—with okra for Southern authenticity. Corn or lima beans can be substituted, if you prefer.

Boneless, skinless turkey thighs, cut into 1 1/2 inch (3.8 cm) pieces	2 lbs.	900 g
Southwest no-salt seasoning	1 tbsp.	15 mL
Canola oil	2 tsp.	10 mL
Dry (or alcohol-free) white wine	1/2 cup	125 mL
Red baby potatoes, quartered	2 lbs.	900 g
28 oz. (796 mL) can of diced tomatoes (with juice)	1	1
Cajun seasoning	1 tbsp.	15 mL
Chopped fresh (or frozen, thawed) okra	2 cups	500 mL
Chopped onion	1 1/2 cups	375 mL
Chopped green pepper	1 cup	250 mL
Chopped celery	1 cup	250 mL
Cajun seasoning	1 tbsp.	15 mL

Combine turkey and first amount of Cajun seasoning in a medium bowl, stirring until turkey is coated. Heat oil in a large frying pan on medium-high. Cook turkey, in 2 batches, for about 5 minutes, stirring occasionally, until browned. Transfer to a 4 to 5 quart (4 to 5 L) slow cooker.

Add wine to same frying pan. Heat, stirring and scraping any brown bits from bottom of pan, until boiling. Add to slow cooker.

Stir in next 7 ingredients. Cook, covered, on Low for 8 to 10 hours, or on High for 4 to 5 hours.

Stir in remaining Cajun seasoning. Serves 6.

1 serving: 380 Calories; 10 g Total Fat (4 g Mono, 2 g Poly, 2.5 g Sat); 100 mg Cholesterol; 39 g Carbohydrate (5 g Fibre, 6 g Sugar); 35 g Protein; 160 mg Sodium

Coq au Vin

The classic French dish gets a slow cooker makeover in this delicious recipe.

Bacon slices, diced	3	3
All-purpose flour	1/4 cup	60 mL
Paprika	1/4 tsp.	1 mL
Boneless, skinless chicken legs (about 3 oz., 85 g, each)	6	6
Boneless, skinless chicken breasts (about 4 oz., 113 g each), cut in half	3	3
Fresh white mushrooms	4 cups	1 L
Baby carrots	1 cup	250 mL
Chopped onion	1 cup	250 mL
Garlic clove, minced (or 1/4 tsp., 1 mL, powder)	1	1
10 oz. (284 mL) can of condensed, low-sodium cream of mushroom soup	1	1
Dry (or alcohol-free) red wine	1/2 cup	125 mL
Prepared chicken broth	1/2 cup	125 mL
Bay leaves	2	2
Dried thyme	1/2 tsp.	2 mL

Chopped fresh parsley, for garnish (optional)

Cook bacon in a large frying pan on medium until crisp. Transfer with a slotted spoon to a plate lined with paper towel to drain. Set aside.

Heat 1 tbsp. (15 mL) drippings in same frying pan on medium. Combine flour and paprika in a large resealable freezer bag. Add half of chicken. Seal bag and toss until chicken is coated. Repeat with remaining chicken. Discard any remaining flour mixture. Add chicken to frying pan in 2 batches. Cook for 8 to 10 minutes per batch, turning occasionally, until browned. Transfer to 3 1/2 to 4 quart (3.5 to 4 L) slow cooker.

Add next 3 ingredients to same frying pan. Cook for about 2 minutes, scraping any brown bits from bottom of pan, until onion starts to soften.

Add next 5 ingredients and bacon. Heat, stirring, for about 2 minutes until mixture just starts to boil. Pour over chicken. Cook, covered, on Low for 7 to 8 hours, or on High for 3 1/2 to 4 hours. Discard bay leaves. Transfer chicken mixture to a serving platter.

Garnish with parsley. Serves 6.

1 serving: 380 Calories; 16 g Total Fat (6 g Mono, 3 g Poly, 4.5 g Sat); 105 mg Cholesterol; 12 g Carbohydrate (1 g Fibre, 4 g Sugar); 43 g Protein; 370 mg Sodium

Cajun Chicken

Got a ragin' Cajun hunger? With a pot of this hearty sausage and chicken stew, Mardi Gras is just a slow cooker away. Serve over rice.

Chopped onion	1 1/2 cups	375 mL
Chopped red pepper	1 cup	250 mL
Chopped celery	1/3 cup	75 mL
Garlic cloves, minced	4	4
(or 1 tsp., 5 mL, powder)		
All-purpose flour	2 tbsp.	30 mL
Sliced green onion	1/3 cup	75 mL
10 oz. (285 g) lean kielbasa (or smoked ham)	1	1
sausage ring, cut into 6 pieces		
and halved lengthwise		
Boneless, skinless chicken thighs	10	10
(about 3 oz., 85 g, each)		
Bay leaf	1	1
Prepared low-sodium chicken broth	1 cup	250 mL
Chili sauce	1/2 cup	125 mL
Chili powder	1 1/2 tsp.	7 mL
Dried basil	1/2 tsp.	2 mL
Dried oregano	1/2 tsp.	2 mL
Ground thyme	1/4 tsp.	1 mL
Pepper	1/4 tsp.	1 mL

Mix first 4 ingredients together. Transfer to a 4 to 5 quart (4 to 5 L) slow cooker. Sprinkle with flour.

Layer next 3 ingredients, in order given, over vegetable mixture. Add bay leaf.

Combine next 7 ingredients in a medium bowl and pour over chicken. Cook, covered, on Low for 7 to 8 hours, or on High for 3 1/2 to 4 hours. Remove bay leaf. Serves 6.

1 serving: 300 Calories; 8 g Total Fat (2 g Mono, 1.5 g Poly, 2.5 g Sat); 104 mg Cholesterol; 20 g Carbohydrate (2 g Fibre, 9 g Sugar); 35 g Protein; 850 mg Sodium

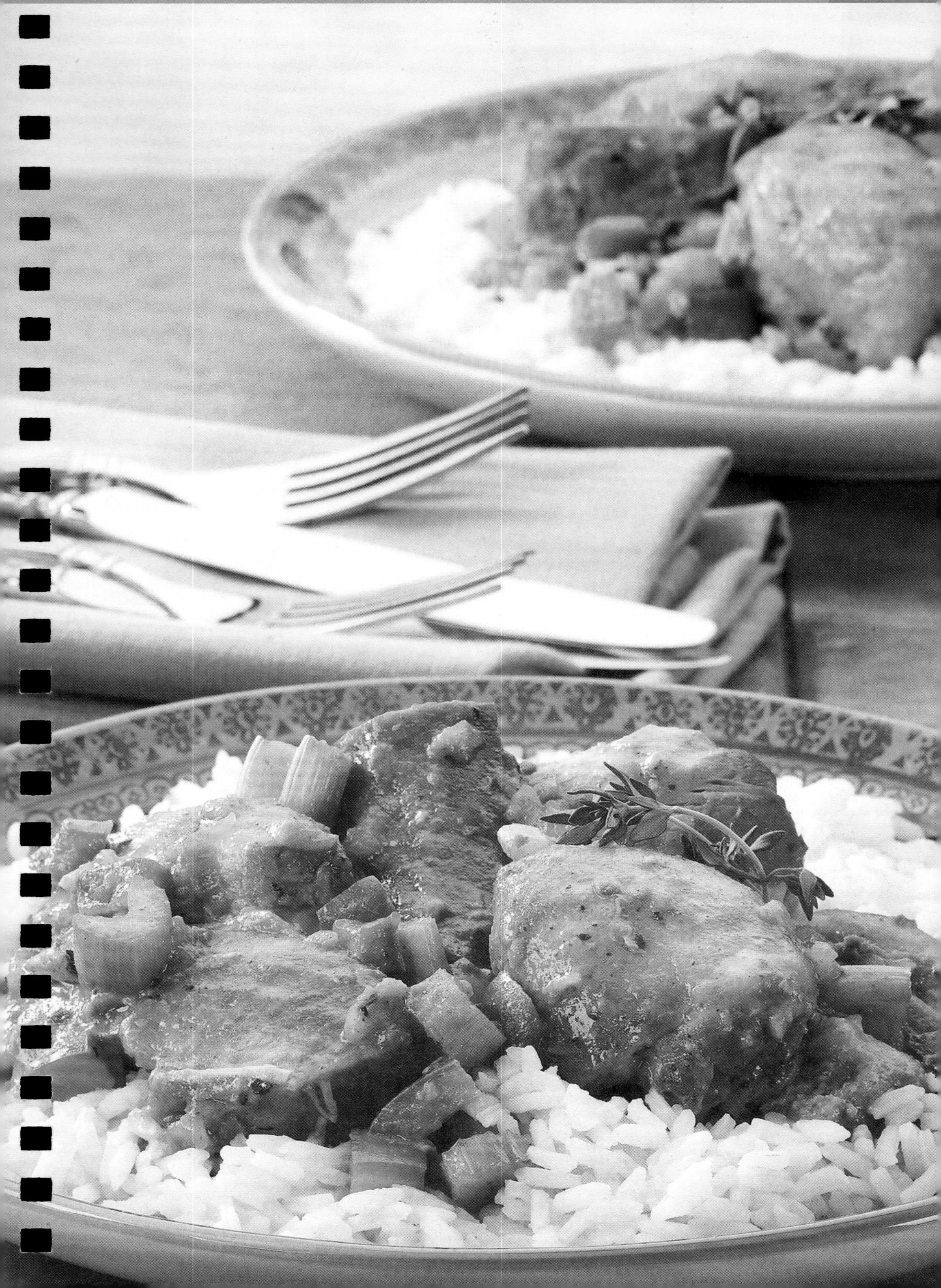

Buffalo Chicken Casserole

Spicy chicken stew with a delicious blue cheese biscuit topping. Serve with beer and your sport of choice!

Boneless, skinless chicken thighs, halved	2 lbs.	900 g
Chopped onion	1 cup	250 mL
Garlic cloves, minced	2	2
(or 1/2 tsp., 2 mL, powder)		
Salt	1/4 tsp.	1 mL
Pepper	1/8 tsp.	0.5 mL
All-purpose flour	3 tbsp.	45 mL
Prepared low-sodium chicken broth	1 cup	250 mL
Louisiana hot sauce	1/4 cup	60 mL
Sliced baby potato	2 cups	500 mL
Sliced carrot	1 1/2 cups	375 mL
Sliced celery	1 cup	250 mL
Biscuit mix	2 cups	500 mL
Crumbled blue cheese	3 tbsp.	45 mL
Chopped fresh parsley	2 tbsp.	30 mL
(or 1 tsp., 5 mL, flakes)		
Milk	1 cup	250 mL

Combine first 5 ingredients in a 4 quart (4 L) slow cooker.

Combine flour, broth and hot sauce in a medium cup, stirring until smooth. Add to chicken. Stir in next 3 ingredients. Cook, covered, on Low for 6 to 7 hours, or on High for 3 to 4 hours.

For the biscuits, combine next 3 ingredients in a medium bowl. Make a well in centre.

Add milk. Stir until just moistened. Drop batter onto hot chicken mixture in 8 mounds, using about 1/4 cup (60 mL) for each. Cook, covered, on High for 30 to 40 minutes until wooden pick inserted in centre of biscuit comes out clean. Serves 8.

1 serving: 400 Calories; 12.5 g Total Fat (2 g Mono, 1.5 g Poly, 3.5 g Sat); 100 mg Cholesterol; 48 g Carbohydrate (3 g Fibre, 5 g Sugar); 29 g Protein; 850 mg Sodium

Slow Cooker Pheasant

Slow cookers are ideal for cooking wild pheasant—as well as other game birds—because the meat requires a slow cook on low heat to keep from drying out. Pheasant does not have a strong gamey taste, and you can leave the skin on for more flavour, if you prefer. If you are purchasing commercially raised pheasant, younger birds are the best choice for a moist, succulent meal.

Water	1/2 cup	125 mL
Salt	1/4 cup	60 mL
Pheasants, bones and skin removed, rinsed, patted dry and cut into large pieces	2	2
Low-sodium soy sauce	1/4 cup	60 mL
Low-sodium chicken broth	3 tbsp.	45 mL
Worcestershire sauce	2 tbsp.	30 mL
Balsamic vinegar	2 tbsp.	30 mL
Brown sugar	3 tbsp.	45 mL
Minced garlic	2 tbsp.	30 mL
Hot pepper sauce	1 tbsp.	15 mL
Ground thyme	2 tsp.	10 mL
Cooking oil	2 tsp.	10 mL
Chopped onion	2 cups	500 mL
Quartered mushrooms	2 cups	500 mL
Water	1/2 cup	125 mL
Fresh thyme sprigs	3	3
Chopped fresh thyme	2 tbsp.	30 mL

Combine first amount of water and salt in a large bowl. Add pheasant pieces and soak for 1 hour.

In a small bowl, mix together next 8 ingredients. Remove pheasant from salt water and place in a large resealable plastic bag. Pour in marinade, seal bag and refrigerate for at least 2 hours.

Heat oil in a medium frying pan on medium. Add onion and mushroom. Cook until onion is soft and liquid from mushrooms is evaporated. Add to a 4 to 5 quart (4 to 5 L) slow cooker.

Transfer pheasant pieces to slow cooker and discard marinade. Add second amount of water and thyme. Cook, covered, on Low for 7 to 8 hours, or on High for 3 1/2 to 4 hours. Remove thyme sprigs.

Garnish with fresh thyme. Serves 8.

1 serving: 270 Calories; 8 g Total Fat (3 g Mono, 1.5 g Poly, 2.5 g Sat); 115 mg Cholesterol; 6 g Carbohydrate (trace Fibre, 4 g Sugar); 43 g Protein; 520 mg Sodium

Chicken Marrakesh

Bring the flavours of Morocco into your kitchen with this satisfying blend of quinoa, tender chicken and earthy spices.

Olive oil	1 tbsp.	15 mL
Boneless, skinless chicken thighs, trimmed fat, halved	2 lbs.	900 g
Salt	1/2 tsp.	2 mL
Pepper	1/4 tsp.	1 mL
Chopped red pepper	2 cups	500 mL
Sliced leek, white part only	1 cup	250 mL
Garlic clove, minced	2	2
Ground cumin	1 1/2 tsp.	7 mL
Ground cinnamon	1/2 tsp.	2 mL
Ground ginger	1/2 tsp.	2 mL
No-salt seasoning	1/2 tsp.	2 mL
Cayenne pepper	1/8 tsp.	0.5 mL
Dry (or alcohol-free) white wine	1/2 cup	125 mL
Prepared low-sodium chicken broth	2 cups	500 mL
Quinoa, rinsed and drained	1/2 cup	125 mL
Orange juice	3/4 cup	175 mL
Dried apricots, chopped	1/2 cup	125 mL
Green onion, sliced	1/4 cup	60 mL
Almonds, sliced and toasted	1/4 cup	60 mL

Heat oil in a large frying pan on medium-high. Add chicken and sprinkle with salt and pepper. Cook, stirring occasionally, for about 8 minutes until browned. Transfer with a slotted spoon to a 3 1/2 to 4 quart (3.5 to 4 L) slow cooker. Reduce heat to medium.

Add next 3 ingredients to same frying pan. Cook for about 5 minutes, stirring often, until leek starts to soften. Stir in next 5 ingredients and heat until it becomes fragrant. About 2 minutes. Add wine. Heat, stirring and scraping any brown bits from bottom of pan, until boiling. Add to slow cooker.

Stir in next 4 ingredients. Cook, covered, on Low for about 3 to 4 hours, or on High for 1 1/2 to 2 hours.

Stir in green onions and almonds. Serves 4.

1 serving: 390 Calories; 12 g Total Fat (6 g Mono, 2.5 g Poly, 2 g Sat); 95 mg Cholesterol; 38 g Carbohydrate (6 g Fibre, 14 g Sugar); 30 g Protein; 740 mg Sodium

Chicken with Vegetable Hash

Put the root vegetables from your garden to good use in this colourful dish.
A perfect meal for the cooler days of autumn.

Chopped carrots	2 cups	500 mL
Chopped parsnips	2 cups	500 mL
Peeled, chopped butternut squash	2 cups	500 mL
Peeled. chopped turnip	1 cup	250 mL
Leek, sliced white part only	1 cup	250 mL
Boneless, skinless chicken thighs	12	12
Salt	1 tsp.	5 mL
Pepper	1 tsp.	5 mL
Prepared low-sodium chicken broth	1 1/2 cups	375 mL
Tomato paste (see Tip, page 18)	2 tbsp.	30 mL
Bay leaves	2	2
Paprika	1 tsp.	5 mL
Dried thyme	1 tsp.	5 mL
Chopped fresh thyme	3 tbsp.	45 mL

Combine first 5 ingredients in a 6 to 7 quart (6 to 7 L) slow cooker.

Season chicken thighs with salt and pepper and place on top of vegetables.

Whisk together next 5 ingredients in a medium bowl. Pour over chicken mixture. Cook, covered, on Low for 7 to 8 hours, or on High for 3 to 4 hours.

Top with fresh thyme. Serves 6.

1 serving: 270 Calories; 6 g Total Fat (2 g Mono, 1.5 g Poly, 1.5 g Sat); 95 mg Cholesterol; 29 g Carbohydrate (6 g Fibre, 9 g Sugar); 26 g Protein; 530 mg Sodium

Tipsy Chicken and Olives

A great dish to eat during winter. Serve over cooked brown rice to soak up the tasty gravy.

Canola oil	2 tsp.	10 mL
Boneless, skinless chicken breasts, (about 4 oz.,113 g, each), cut in half	4	4
Sliced onion	1 cup	250 mL
Sliced shallot, sliced	1/2 cup	125 mL
Chopped celery	1 cup	250 mL
Chopped carrot	1 cup	250 mL
Garlic cloves, minced	2	2
Pale ale	1 cup	250 mL
Prepared low-sodium chicken broth	1 1/2 cups	375 mL
Frozen peas	1 cup	250 mL
Fresh rosemary sprigs	2	2
Garlic and herb no-salt seasoning	1 tsp.	5 mL
Pepper	1/2 tsp.	2 mL
Green olives pitted	1 cup	250 mL
Chopped fresh rosemary	2 tbsp.	30 mL

Heat oil in a large frying pan on medium-high. Add chicken. Cook for about 8 minutes, stirring occasionally, until browned on all sides. Transfer with a slotted spoon to a 4 to 5 quart (4 to 5 L) slow cooker.

Add next 5 ingredients to same frying pan. Cook for about 5 minutes, stirring often, until onion starts to soften.

Add beer, scraping any browned bits from bottom of pot. Transfer to slow cooker.

Stir in next 5 ingredients. Cook, covered, on Low for 7 to 8 hours, or on High for 3 1/2 to 4 hours.

Discard rosemary sprigs and add green olives and fresh rosemary. Serves 4.

1 serving: 340 Calories; 7 g Total Fat (3.5 g Mono, 1 g Poly, 0.5 g Sat); 85 mg Cholesterol; 25 g Carbohydrate (3 g Fibre, 8 g Sugar); 41 g Protein; 900 mg Sodium

Chicken Mole

Not the prettiest dish you'll ever make, but the flavour is spectacular. Mole sauces are some of Mexico's signature dishes. Serve with rice and an ice-cold beer, or tear the chicken and stuff it into corn tortillas.

Boneless, skinless chicken breast (about 4 oz., 113 g, each)	8	8
No-salt seasoning	1 tsp.	5 mL
Pepper	1/2 tsp.	2 mL
28 oz. (796 mL) canned whole tomatoes, with juice	1	1
Prepared low-sodium chicken broth	1/2 cup	125 mL
Diced onion	3/4 cup	175 mL
1 oz. (28 g) square of bittersweet chocolate, finely chopped	1	1
Sesame seeds	3 tbsp.	45 mL
Chopped chipotle peppers in adobo sauce (see Tip, page 44)	1 1/2 tbsp.	22 mL
Dried ancho chili peppers, stemmed, seeded and cut in half	3	3
Garlic cloves, sliced	3	3
Olive oil	2 tbsp.	30 mL
Raisins	2 tbsp.	30 mL
Chipotle chili powder	1 tbsp.	15 mL
Ground cumin	1 tsp.	5 mL
Dried oregano	1/2 tsp.	2 mL
Chopped fresh cilantro	1/4 cup	60 mL
Sesame seeds, toasted (optional)	2 tsp.	10 mL
Lime wedges (optional)	4	4

Sprinkle both sides of chicken with salt and pepper and place in a 3 1/2 to 4 quart (3.5 to 4 L) slow cooker.

Place next 13 ingredients into a blender and blend until smooth. Pour over chicken and stir. Cook, covered, on Low for 8 hours, or on High for 4 hours.

Stir in cilantro and second amount of sesame seed. Serve with lime wedges. Serves 4.

1 serving: 390 Calories; 20 g Total Fat (7 g Mono, 3.5 g Poly, 4 g Sat); 80 mg Cholesterol; 30 g Carbohydrate (8 g Fibre, 13 g Sugar); 31 g Protein; 660 mg Sodium

Cashew Chicken

Although cashew chicken is traditionally cooked in a wok, this recipe gives you all the flavour of the original with the convenience of using a slow cooker. Tastes great with rice or noodles.

Chicken drumsticks, skin removed	12	12
Prepared low-sodium chicken stock	1/2 cup	125 mL
Low-sodium soy sauce	1/2 cup	125 mL
Hoisin sauce	1/4 cup	60 mL
Rice wine vinegar	1/4 cup	60 mL
Sesame oil	1 1/2 tbsp.	22 mL
Grated ginger root	2 tsp.	10 mL
Pepper	1 tsp.	5 mL
Sliced orange pepper	1 cup	250 mL
Sliced yellow pepper	1 cup	250 mL
Sliced onion	1 cup	250 mL
Chopped unsalted cashews	1 cup	250 mL
All-purpose flour	2 tbsp.	15 mL

Arrange drumsticks in a 3 1/2 to 4 quart (3.5 to 4 L) slow cooker.

Combine next 7 ingredients in a medium bowl. Remove 1/2 cup (125 mL) liquid and set aside. Pour remaining mixture over chicken. Arrange next 4 ingredients over top. Cook, covered, on Low for 5 to 6 hours, or on High for 2 1/2 to 3 hours.

Combine reserved liquid with flour, mixing well. Stir into mixture in slow cooker. Cook, covered, on High for 20 minutes. Serves 6.

1 serving: 350 Calories; 19 g Total Fat (3 g Mono, 3 g Poly, 4 g Sat); 85 mg Cholesterol; 17 g Carbohydrate (2 g Fibre, 4 g Sugar); 26 g Protein; 750 mg Sodium

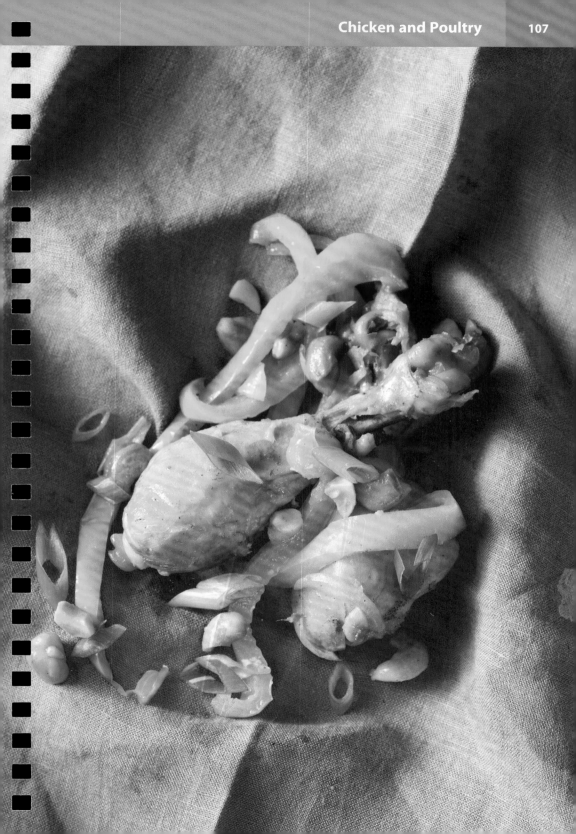

Cranberry Apricot Stuffed Turkey Breasts

This elegant turkey, with its cranberry apricot stuffing, is truly impressive. Serve with roasted or mashed potatoes.

Fresh white bread cubes (crusts removed), about 4 slices	3 cups	750 mL
Finely chopped onion	2/3 cup	150 mL
Finely chopped dried cranberries	1/4 cup	60 mL
Finely chopped dried apricots	1/4 cup	60 mL
Chopped fresh sage (or 1 1/2 tsp., 7 mL, dried)	2 tbsp.	30 mL
Orange marmalade	2 tbsp.	30 mL
Dry mustard	1 tsp.	5 mL
Salt	1/4 tsp.	1 mL
Pepper	1/2 tsp.	2 mL
Boneless, skinless turkey breast roasts (about 1.5 lbs, 680 g, each)	2	2
Cooking oil	2 tsp.	10 mL
Salt, sprinkle		
Prepared low-sodium chicken broth	3/4 cup	175 mL
Apricot jam	1/4 cup	60 mL
Cornstarch	1 tbsp.	15 mL
Orange juice	1 cup	250 mL
Water	1/3 cup	75 mL
Dijon mustard	1 tbsp.	15 mL

For the stuffing, spread bread cubes in a single layer on an ungreased baking sheet. Bake in a 250°F (120°C) oven for about 15 minutes, stirring occasionally, until dried. Transfer to a large bowl.

Add next 8 ingredients. Stir well. Set aside.

To butterfly roasts, cut each horizontally lengthwise, almost but not quite through to other side. Press open to flatten. Place between 2 pieces of plastic wrap. Pound with a mallet or rolling pin to 3/4 inch (2 cm) thickness. Remove and discard plastic wrap. Spread each roast with half of cranberry stuffing, leaving a 1 inch (2.5 cm) edge along top. Roll up jelly-roll style to enclose filling. Tie with butcher's string or secure with metal skewers.

Brush roasts with cooking oil. Sprinkle with salt. Place in a 6 to 7 quart (6 to 7 L) slow cooker. Pour stock over roasts. Cook, covered, on Low for 8 to 10 hours, or on High for 4 to 5 hours.

Meanwhile, combine apricot jam and cornstarch in a saucepan. Stir in remaining 3 ingredients until smooth. Bring to a boil. Cook, stirring, for about 4 minutes until thickened. Brush liberally over roasts and cook on High for 30 minutes. Cover with foil. Let stand for 10 minutes. Internal temperature should rise to at least 160°F (70ºC). Serves 10.

1 serving: 380 Calories; 14 g Total Fat (5 g Mono, 3.5 g Poly, 3.5 g Sat); 100 mg Cholesterol; 22 g Carbohydrate (1 g Fibre, 12 g Sugar); 41 g Protein; 240 mg Sodium

Sweet and Spicy Seafood Stew

The combination of spices and subtle sweetness in this lazy stew fills your kitchen with a tantalizing aroma. Do not add the seafood too early.

Potatoes, peeled and diced	2 lbs.	900 g
Yellow turnip (rutabaga), peeled and diced	1 lb.	454 g
Sliced carrots	1 lb.	454 g
Tomato sauce	3 cups	750 mL
Ketchup	1/4 cup	60 mL
Honey	2 tbsp.	30 mL
Dijon mustard	1 tbsp.	15 mL
Molasses	1 tbsp.	15 mL
Italian seasoning	2 tsp.	10 mL
Minced garlic	1 1/2 tsp.	7 mL
Turmeric	1 1/2 tsp.	7 mL
Cayenne pepper	1 tsp.	5 mL
Herb and garlic no-salt seasoning	3/4 tsp.	4 mL
Water	1 1/2 cups	375 mL
Large sea scallops	1 lb.	454 g
Uncooked medium shrimp (peeled and deveined)	1 lb.	454 g
Cornstarch (optional)	2 tbsp.	30 mL

Combine first 13 ingredients in a 5 to 6 quart (5 to 6 L) slow cooker. Cook, covered, on Low for 5 hours, or on High for 3 to 4 hours.

Stir in water, scallops and shrimp. Add cornstarch for a thicker consistency. Cook, covered, on High for 15 to 20 minutes until shrimp are pink. Serves 7.

1 serving: 400 Calories; 2.5 g Total Fat (0 g Mono, 0 g Poly, 1 g Sat); 100 mg Cholesterol; 62 g Carbohydrate (7 g Fibre, 22 g Sugar); 34 g Protein; 1000 mg Sodium

Seafood Quinoa Jambalaya

A nicely textured jambalaya with nutritious quinoa and sweet, tender seafood. The heat is very mild, so add more cayenne for a hotter dish. If you are not a fan of quinoa, use rice instead.

Canola oil	2 tsp.	10 mL
Chopped onion	1 1/2 cups	375 mL
Chopped celery	1 cup	250 mL
Tomato paste (see Tip, page 18)	2 tbsp.	30 mL
Chili powder	2 tsp.	10 mL
Garlic cloves, minced	2	2
Dried oregano	1 tsp.	5 mL
Dried thyme	1 tsp.	5 mL
No-salt seasoning	1/8 tsp.	0.5 mL
Pepper	1/2 tsp.	2 mL
Cayenne pepper	1/4 tsp.	1 mL
Prepared low-sodium chicken broth	2 cups	500 mL
Dry (or alcohol-free) white wine	1 cup	250 mL
Quinoa, rinsed and drained	1 1/2 cups	375 mL
Small bay scallops	1/2 lb.	225 g
Uncooked medium shrimp (peeled and deveined)	1/2 lb.	225 g
Chopped green pepper	3/4 cup	175 mL
Chopped seeded tomato	3/4 cup	175 mL
Chopped yellow pepper	3/4 cup	175 mL
Frozen peas	3/4 cup	175 mL

Heat canola oil in a large frying pan on medium. Add onion and celery. Cook for about 10 minutes, stirring often, until softened.

Add next 8 ingredients. Heat, stirring, for about 1 minute until fragrant.

Add 1 cup (250 mL) broth and wine. Heat, stirring, until boiling. Transfer to 3 1/2 to 4 quart (3.5 to 4 L) slow cooker. Stir in quinoa and remaining broth. Cook, covered, on Low for 4 to 5 hours, or on High for 2 to 2 1/2 hours.

Stir in remaining 6 ingredients. Cook, covered, on High for about 20 minutes until peppers are tender-crisp and shrimp turn pink. Serves 6.

1 serving: *300 Calories; 4.5 g Total Fat (1 g Mono, 1 g Poly, 0 g Sat); 70 mg Cholesterol; 38 g Carbohydrate (5 g Fibre, 5 g Sugar); 22 g Protein; 410 mg Sodium*

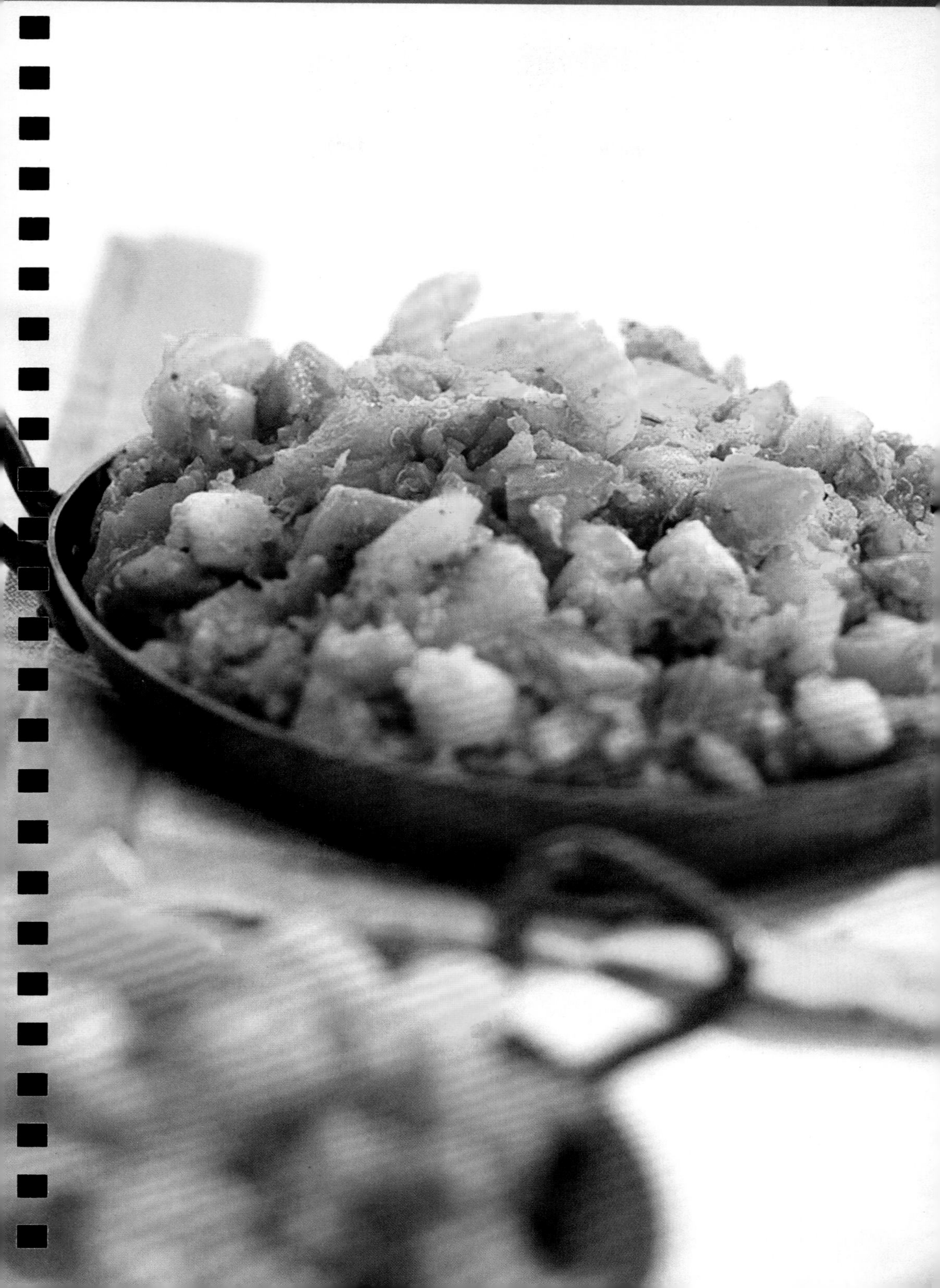

Fish Burritos

Tilapia, black bean and corn burritos served with a fresh pineapple salsa. Delicious!

19 oz. (540 mL) can of black beans, rinsed and drained	1	1
Sliced onion	1 1/2 cups	375 mL
Fresh (or frozen, thawed) kernel corn	1 cup	250 mL
Lime juice	1 tbsp.	15 mL
Chopped pickled pepper rings	2 tsp.	10 mL
Chili powder	1 tsp.	5 mL
Ground cumin	1/2 tsp.	2 mL
Garlic clove, minced	1	1
Salt	1/8 tsp.	0.5 mL
Pepper	1/4 tsp.	1 mL
Thinly sliced red pepper	1 cup	250 mL
Thinly sliced yellow pepper	1 cup	250 mL
Tilapia fillets, any small bones removed	3/4 lb.	340 g
Diced pineapple	1 cup	250 mL
Diced radishes	1/2 cup	125 mL
Chopped cilantro	2 tbsp.	30 mL
Lime juice	1 tbsp.	15 mL
Whole wheat flour tortillas (8 inch, 20 cm, diameter)	8	8
Shredded romaine lettuce, lightly packed	1 cup	250 mL
Chopped seeded tomato	1/2 cup	125 mL
Grated jalapeño Monterey Jack cheese	1/2 cup	125 mL
Finely chopped green onion	2 tbsp.	30 mL

Combine first 10 ingredients in a 3 1/2 to 4 quart (3.5 to 4 L) slow cooker. Cook, covered, on Low for 4 to 5 hours, or on High for 2 to 2 1/2 hours.

Stir in red and yellow pepper. Arrange fillets over top. Cook, covered, on High for about 25 minutes until fish flakes easily when tested with a fork.

As the fish is cooking, prepare pineapple salsa by combining pineapple, radish, cilantro and lime juice. Let stand for 30 minutes.

Grill tortillas on medium heat for 2 minutes per side. Transfer fillets to a large plate. Break into small pieces with a fork. Arrange black bean mixture down centre of each tortilla. Top with fish and remaining 4 ingredients. Fold sides over filling. Roll up from bottom to enclose filling. Serve with pineapple salsa. Makes 8 burritos.

1 serving: *350 Calories; 7 g Total Fat (2 g Mono, 0.5 g Poly, 2 g Sat); 30 mg Cholesterol; 51 g Carbohydrate (7 g Fibre, 5 g Sugar); 21 g Protein; 480 mg Sodium*

Indian Fish Curry

This vibrant coconut curry has a gentle heat and pairs perfectly with brown rice. Garnish with Thai basil.

Butter	1 tbsp.	15 mL
Chopped onion	2 cups	500 mL
Sliced mushrooms	2 cups	500 mL
Curry powder	2 tbsp.	30 mL
Finely grated ginger root	2 tsp.	10 mL
(or 1/2 tsp., 2 mL, ground ginger)		
Garlic cloves, minced	2	2
(or 1/2 tsp., 2 mL, powder)		
Cauliflower florets, halved	1 1/2 cups	375 mL
Diced unpeeled potato	1 1/2 cups	375 mL
Light coconut milk	1 cup	250 mL
Prepared vegetable broth	1 cup	250 mL
Unsweetened applesauce	1 cup	250 mL
Brown sugar, packed	2 tsp.	10 mL
Cayenne pepper	1/4 tsp.	1 mL
Salt	1/4 tsp.	1 mL
Crushed red pepper flakes	1/4 tsp.	1 mL
Halibut fillets, any small bones removed,	1 lb.	454 g
cut into 1 inch (2.5 cm) pieces		
Chopped fresh spinach leaves,	1 cup	250 mL
lightly packed		
Chopped tomato	1 cup	250 mL
Sliced, seeded Thai chilies	2 tsp.	10 mL

Melt butter in a large frying pan on medium. Add onion amd mushrooms. Cook for about 10 minutes, stirring often, until onion is softened and liquid from mushrooms is evaporated.

Add next 3 ingredients. Heat, stirring, for about 1 minute until fragrant. Transfer to a 3 1/2 to 4 quart (3.5 to 4 L) slow cooker.

Stir in next 9 ingredients. Cook, covered, on Low for 5 to 6 hours, or on High for 2 1/2 to 3 hours.

Add remaining 4 ingredients. Cook, covered, on High for about 30 minutes until fish flakes easily when tested with a fork. Sprinkle with Thai chilies. Serves 6.

1 serving: 250 Calories; 7 g Total Fat (1 g Mono, 1 g Poly, 3.5 g Sat); 30 mg Cholesterol; 28 g Carbohydrate (5 g Fibre, 12 g Sugar); 20 g Protein; 290 mg Sodium

South Asian Steamed Salmon

A whole meal in one dish! Tender salmon is slowly steamed on a bed of spicy, flavourful barley and veggies.

Prepared low-sodium vegetable broth	2 cups	500 mL
Chopped onion	1 cup	250 mL
Diced carrot	1 cup	250 mL
Pot barley	1 cup	250 mL
Water	1 cup	250 mL
Chopped pickled pepper rings	3 tbsp.	45 mL
Sesame oil (for flavour)	1 tsp.	5 mL
Garlic clove, minced (or 1/4 tsp., 1 mL, powder)	1	1
Halved sugar snap peas, trimmed	1 cup	250 mL
Salmon fillets, skin and any small bones removed	1 lb.	454 g
Rice vinegar	1/4 cup	60 mL
Granulated sugar	2 tsp.	10 mL
Roasted sesame seeds	1 tbsp.	15 mL

Combine first 8 ingredients in a greased 4 to 5 quart (4 to 5 L) slow cooker. Cook, covered, on Low for 4 to 5 hours, or on High for 2 to 2 1/2 hours.

Stir in peas. Arrange fillets over barley mixture.

Combine vinegar and sugar in small bowl stirring until sugar is dissolved. Drizzle over fillets. Cook, covered, on High for about 20 minutes until fish flakes easily when tested with fork.

Sprinkle with sesame seeds. Serves 4.

1 serving: 400 Calories; 10 g Total Fat (3 g Mono, 4 g Poly, 1.5 g Sat); 60 mg Cholesterol; 49 g Carbohydrate (9 g Fibre, 10 g Sugar); 28 g Protein; 510 mg Sodium

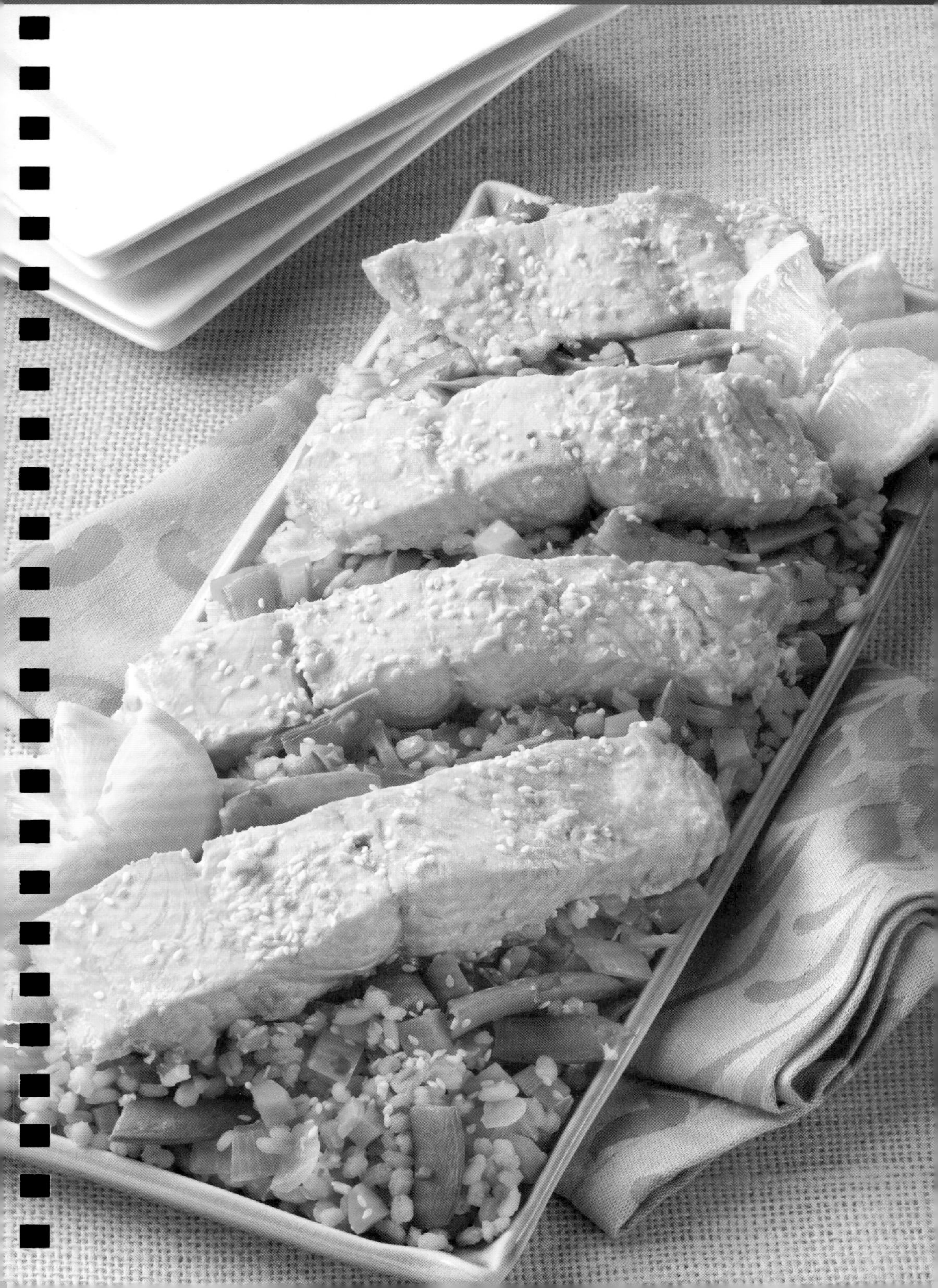

Herbed Seafood Risotto

A colourful, delicately textured risotto with rich herb flavour, a hint of citrus and perfectly tender seafood. Full-flavour impact in a light main course.

Canola oil	1 tsp.	5 mL
Chopped fennel bulb (white part only)	1 cup	250 mL
Chopped onion	1 cup	250 mL
Garlic cloves, minced	2	2
Dry white wine (alcohol-free)	3/4 cup	175 mL
Prepared vegetable broth	2 cups	500 mL
Diced red pepper	1 1/2 cups	375 mL
Diced yellow pepper	1 1/2 cups	375 mL
Arborio rice	1 cup	250 mL
Diced zucchini (with peel)	1 cup	250 mL
Dried basil	1 tsp.	5 mL
Dried dillweed	1 tsp.	5 mL
Small bay scallops	1/2 lb.	225 g
Haddock fillet, any small bones removed	1/2 lb.	225 g
Chopped fresh parsley (or 1 1/2 tsp., 7 mL, flakes)	3 tbsp.	45 mL
Grated Parmesan cheese	3 tbsp.	45 mL
Lemon juice	2 tbsp.	30 mL
Grated lemon zest	1 tsp.	5 mL
Pepper	1/2 tsp.	2 mL

Heat canola oil in a large frying pan on medium. Add next 3 ingredients. Cook for about 8 minutes, stirring often, until fennel is softened. Add wine and bring to a boil. Cook, stirring, until almost all wine has evaporated, about 4 minutes. Transfer to a 4 to 5 quart (4 to 5 L) slow cooker.

Stir in next 7 ingredients. Cook, covered, on Low for 5 hours, or on High for 2 1/2 hours.

Pour water into a medium saucepan until about 1 inch (2.5 cm) deep. Bring to a boil. Add scallops. Cook, uncovered, for about 1 minute until scallops turn opaque. Transfer with a slotted spoon to rice mixture.

Add fillet to same pot. Cook, uncovered, for about 2 minutes until fish flakes easily when tested with a fork. Transfer with slotted spoon to a large plate. Break into small pieces with a fork. Add to rice mixture.

Gently stir in remaining 5 ingredients. Serves 5.

1 serving: 320 Calories; 3 g Total Fat (1 g Mono, 0.5 g Poly, 1 g Sat); 45 mg Cholesterol; 44 g Carbohydrate (3 g Fibre, 5 g Sugar); 22 g Protein; 400 mg Sodium

Salmon Cabbage Rolls

This tasty twist on tradition adds salmon and pot barley to the cabbage rolls' rice filling, and has an onion cream sauce in place of the tomato sauce.

Prepared low-sodium chicken broth	4 cups	1 L
Long-grain brown rice	2/3 cup	150 mL
Pot barley	1/3 cup	75 mL
Wild rice	1/3 cup	75 mL
Large head of green cabbage	1	1
Canola oil	1 tsp.	5 mL
Diced onion	1/2 cup	125 mL
Grated carrot	1/4 cup	60 mL
Chopped fresh parsely	1 tbsp.	15 mL
Chopped fresh dill	1 tbsp.	15 mL
Grated lemon zest	1 tsp.	5 mL
Cooked salmon	1 lb.	454 g
Canola oil	1/2 tsp.	2 mL
Chopped onion	1/4 cup	60 mL
Garlic clove, minced	1	1
All-purpose flour	1 tbsp.	15 mL
Skim evaporated milk	1/2 cup	125 mL
Milk	1/3 cup	75 mL
Grated lemon zest	1/2 tsp.	2 mL
Chopped fresh dill (or 1/2 tsp., 2 mL, dried)	2 tsp.	10 mL

Bring broth to a boil in a large saucepan. Stir in next 3 ingredients. Reduce heat to medium-low and simmer, covered, for about 45 minutes until almost tender. Drain, reserving 1 1/3 cups (325 mL) broth. Set aside.

Remove core from cabbage. Trim 1/2 inch (12 mm) slice from bottom. Place, cut side down, in a large pot and cover with boiling water. Cover pot with foil and let stand for 5 minutes. Drain. When cool enough to handle, remove 12 large outer leaves from cabbage. Cut a "V" shape along tough ribs of leaves to remove. Discard ribs. Set leaves aside. Remove another 6 leaves from cabbage. Chop and spread evenly in a 5 to 6 quart (5 to 6 L) slow cooker.

Heat first amount of canola oil in a small frying pan on medium. Add diced onion. Cook for about 5 minutes, stirring often, until softened. Add next 4 ingredients. Heat, stirring, for about 1 minute until fragrant.

In a large bowl, flake salmon with a fork. Add onion mixture and rice mixture. Toss gently. Place about 1/3 cup (75 mL) salmon mixture on each cabbage leaf. Fold in sides. Roll up tightly from bottom to enclose filling. Arrange cabbage rolls, seam side down, over chopped cabbage. Pour reserved broth over cabbage rolls. Cook, covered, on Low for 7 to 8 hours, or on High for 3 1/2 to 4 hours.

For the sauce, heat second amount of oil in a small saucepan on medium. Add chopped onion and garlic. Cook for about 5 minutes, stirring often, until onion is softened. Sprinkle with flour. Heat, stirring, for 1 minute. Slowly add both milks, stirring constantly until smooth. Heat, stirring, for 5 to 10 minutes until boiling and thickened. Remove from heat. Stir in lemon zest and fresh dill. Drizzle over cabbage rolls. Makes 12 cabbage rolls. Serves 6.

1 serving: 400 Calories; 12 g Total Fat
(4 g Mono, 4 g Poly, 2 g Sat); 50 mg
Cholesterol; 50 g Carbohydrate
(7 g Fibre, 13 g Sugar); 28 g
Protein; 560 mg Sodium

Seafood Chowder Casserole

Tender potatoes, creamy sauce and plenty of clams make this the perfect all-in-one meal.

Butter (or hard margarine)	1 tsp.	5 mL
Diced peeled potato (1/2 inch, 12 mm, pieces)	4 cups	1 L
Chopped onion	1 1/2 cups	375 mL
Diced celery	1 cup	250 mL
Bacon slices, chopped	3	3
All-purpose flour	1/4 cup	60 mL
No-salt seasoning	1/2 tsp.	2 mL
Pepper	1/4 tsp.	1 mL
Milk	1 1/2 cups	375 mL
Reserved liquid from clams	1/2 cup	125 mL
Halibut fillets, any small bones removed, cut into 3/4 inch (2 cm) pieces	3/4 lb.	340 g
5 oz. (142 g) can of whole baby clams, drained and liquid reserved	1	1
Crushed round butter-flavoured crackers (about 9 crackers)	1/3 cup	75 mL
Chopped fresh parsley (or 3/4 tsp., 4 mL, flakes)	1 tbsp.	15 mL
Butter (or hard margarine), melted	1 tsp.	5 mL

Melt first amount of butter in Dutch oven on medium. Add next 4 ingredients. Cook for about 12 minutes, stirring often, until celery is softened.

Add next 3 ingredients. Heat and stir for 1 minute. Slowly add milk and clam liquid, stirring constantly until smooth. Heat and stir until boiling and thickened. Remove from heat.

Add fish and clams. Stir. Transfer to greased 3 quart (3 L) casserole. Bake, covered, in 400°F (200°C) oven for about 40 minutes, stirring at halftime, until potato is tender.

Combine remaining 3 ingredients in small bowl. Sprinkle over top. Bake, uncovered, for about 5 minutes until golden. Serves 6.

1 serving: *310 Calories; 11 g Total Fat (3.5 g Mono, 2 g Poly, 3.5 g Sat); 35 mg Cholesterol; 33 g Carbohydrate (2 g Fibre, 7 g Sugar); 20 g Protein; 310 mg Sodium*

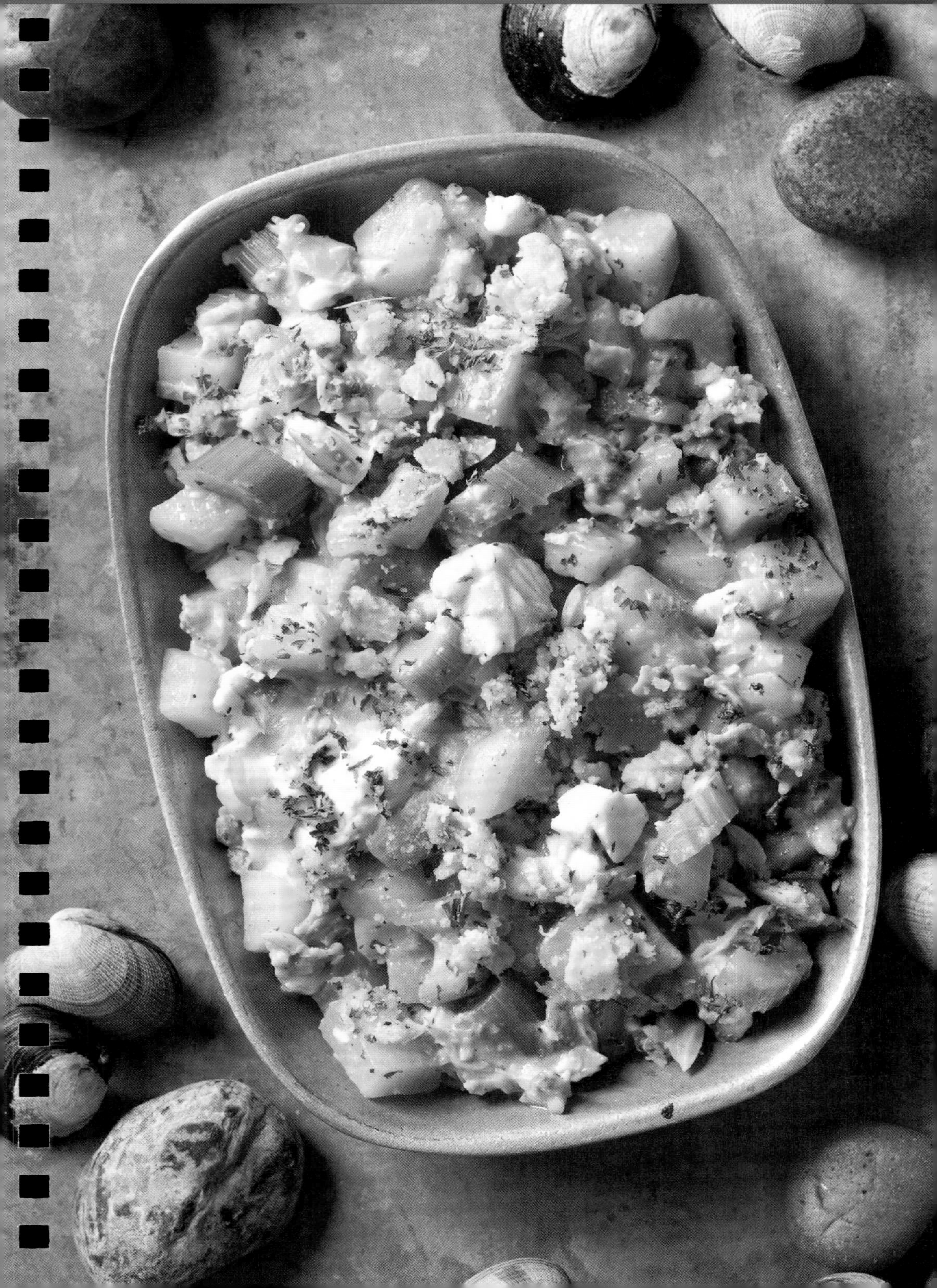

Cioppino

An Italian fish stew, cioppino was traditionally made with whatever was left after the fisherman sold his catch. This version is richly flavoured with wine, lobster, shrimp, scallops and crab.

Medium leeks (white and tender parts only), thinly sliced	2	2
Garlic cloves, minced	3	3
Chopped green pepper	1/2 cup	125 mL
Olive (or cooking) oil	2 tbsp.	30 mL
Butter (or hard margarine)	1 tbsp.	15 mL
Whole small fresh mushrooms (or medium, halved)	3 cups	750 mL
14 oz. (398 mL can of stewed tomatoes (with juice), mashed	1	1
Dry (or alcohol-free) red wine	1 1/2 cups	375 mL
5 1/2 oz. (156 mL) can of tomato paste	1	1
Lemon juice	3 tbsp.	45 mL
Dried sweet basil	2 tsp.	10 mL
Dried thyme	1/2 tsp.	2 mL
Bay leaf	1	1
Uncooked lobster tail (about 8 oz., 225 g), cut into 1 inch (2.5 cm) pieces	1	1
Uncooked medium shrimp (about 8 oz., 225 g), peeled and deveined	24	24
Fresh (or frozen) small bay scallops (about 10 oz., 285 g)	1 1/2 cups	375 mL
King (or snow) crab legs, not shelled, broken into pieces (or 9 oz., 255 g, imitation crab chunks)	1 lb.	454 g
No-salt seasoning	1/2 tsp.	2 mL
Freshly ground pepper, sprinkle		

Sauté leek, garlic and green pepper in olive oil and butter in a large frying pan until leek is soft.

Stir in next 8 ingredients. Bring to a boil. Transfer to a 4 to 5 quart (4 to 5 L) slow cooker. Cook, covered, on Low for 6 to 7 hours, or on High for 3 to 3 1/2 hours. Remove and discard bay leaf.

Stir in remaining 6 ingredients. Cook, covered, on High for 20 to 30 minutes. Serves 6.

1 serving: 290 Calories; 7 g Total Fat (4 g Mono, 0.5 g Poly, 2 g Sat); 95 mg Cholesterol; 19 g Carbohydrate (4 g Fibre, 10 g Sugar); 26 g Protein; 800 mg Sodium

Seafood Chowder

This thick, creamy chowder makes an excellent starter for a dinner party when you want something special for your guests. The thyme adds a fresh accent to the clams and shrimp.

5 oz. (142 g) cans of whole baby clams	2	2
Cooking oil	2 tsp.	10 mL
Chopped onion	2 cups	500 mL
Diced celery	1 cup	250 mL
Garlic cloves, minced	2	2
Diced, peeled baking potato	4 cups	1 L
Prepared low-sodium vegetable broth	5 cups	1.25 L
Bay leaves	2	2
No-salt seasoning	1/2 tsp.	2 mL
Pepper	1/2 tsp.	2 mL
Ground thyme	1/2 tsp.	2 mL
Uncooked medium shrimp, (peeled and deveined)	1/2 lb.	225 g
Evaporated milk	1 1/2 cups	375 mL
Chopped fresh thyme	2 tbsp.	30 mL

Drain clams, reserving 1 cup (250 mL) of liquid. Cover and chill clams.

Heat oil in a large frying pan on medium. Add onion, celery and garlic. Cook for about 10 minutes, stirring often, until softened. Transfer to a 4 to 5 quart (4 to 5 L) slow cooker.

Stir in next 6 ingredients and reserved clam liquid. Cook, covered, on Low for 6 to 7 hours, or on High for 3 to 3 1/2 hours. Break up mixture with a potato masher.

Stir in clams, shrimp, milk and thyme. Cook on High for 20 minutes. Serves 6.

1 serving: 240 Calories; 5 g Total Fat (3 g Mono, 1.5 g Poly, 0.5 g Sat); 60 mg Cholesterol; 32 g Carbohydrate (2 g Fibre, 13 g Sugar); 17 g Protein; 820 mg Sodium

Vegetarian Risotto

This recipe is our tip of the hat to Venice's famous Risi e Bisi, though we've spruced it up with loads of extra vegetables. Serve with your favourite Italian wine.

Canola oil	1 tsp.	5 mL
Chopped leek, white part only	1 cup	250 mL
Chopped onion	1 cup	250 mL
Garlic cloves, minced	2	2
Prepared low-sodium vegetable broth	2 cups	500 mL
Cauliflower, cut in small florets	1 1/2 cups	375 mL
Frozen peas	1 1/2 cups	375 mL
Arborio rice	1 cup	250 mL
Tomatoes, chopped	1 cup	250 mL
Dried basil	1 tsp.	5 mL
Chopped fresh rosemary	3 tbsp.	45 mL
Grated Parmesan	3 tbsp.	45 mL
Lemon juice	2 tbsp.	30 mL
Vermouth	1 tbsp.	15 mL
Grated lemon zest	1 tsp.	5 mL
Pepper	1/2 tsp.	2 mL

Heat canola oil in a large frying pan on medium. Add next 3 ingredients. Cook for about 8 minutes, stirring often, until leeks are softened. Transfer to a 4 to 5 quart (4 to 5 L) slow cooker.

Stir in next 6 ingredients. Cook, covered, on Low for 4 to 5 hours, or on High for 2 1/2 hours.

Gently stir in remaining 6 ingredients. Serves 4.

1 serving: 300 Calories; 3 g Total Fat (1 g Mono, 0.5 g Poly, 1 g Sat); trace Cholesterol; 57 g Carbohydrate (6 g Fibre, 8 g Sugar); 11 g Protein; 480 mg Sodium

Barley Primavera

Creamy and appealing, this dish has a risotto-like texture and lots of colourful, tender-crisp vegetables, with the added nutritional value of barley.

Prepared low-sodium vegetable broth	4 cups	1 L
Pot barley	2 cups	500 mL
Water	2 cups	500 mL
Chopped onion	1 cup	250 mL
Chopped zucchini	2 cups	500 mL
Grape tomatoes, quartered	1 cup	250 mL
Garlic cloves, minced	3	3
Alfredo pasta sauce	1 2/3 cups	400 mL
Chopped fresh basil	3 tbsp.	45 mL

Combine broth, barley and water in a 4 to 5 quart (4 to 5 L) slow cooker. Cook, covered, on Low for 5 to 6 hours, or on High for 2 1/2 to 3 hours until barley is tender and liquid is absorbed.

Stir in next 5 ingredients. Cook, covered, on High for about 30 minutes until vegetables are tender.

Stir in basil. Serves 8.

1 serving: 250 Calories; 6 g Total Fat (0 g Mono, 0 g Poly, 4 g Sat); 20 mg Cholesterol; 42 g Carbohydrate (7 g Fibre, 6 g Sugar); 8 g Protein; 500 mg Sodium

Meatless Moussaka

Lentils take the place of meat in this comforting Greek dish, and we've replaced the traditional béchamel topping with a sprinkle of creamy goat cheese.

19 oz. (540 mL) cans of lentils, rinsed and drained	2	2
Tomato pasta sauce	3 cups	750 mL
Ground cinnamon	1/4 tsp.	1 mL
Salt, to taste		
Pepper, to taste		
Medium eggplants (with peel), cut into 1/4 inch (6 mm) slices	2	2
Goat (chèvre) cheese, crumbled	8 oz.	225 g

Combine first 5 ingredients in a large bowl.

To assemble, layer ingredients in a greased 5 to 7 quart (5 to 7 L) slow cooker as follows:

1. 2 cups (500 mL) lentil mixture

2. Half of eggplant

3. 2 cups (500 mL) lentil mixture

4. Remaining eggplant

5. Remaining lentil mixture

Cook, covered, on Low for 8 to 9 hours, or on High for 4 to 4 1/2 hours.

Sprinkle with cheese. Cook, covered, on High for about 10 minutes until cheese is softened. Serves 6.

1 serving: 370 Calories; 10 g Total Fat (2 g Mono, 0 g Poly, 6 g Sat); 15 mg Cholesterol; 52 g Carbohydrate (16 g Fibre, 11 g Sugar); 21 g Protein; 770 mg Sodium

White Bean Vegetable Chili

This hearty bean chili comes together quickly with ingredients from your pantry and freezer. Serve with tortilla chips or corn bread, or use it as a taco filling.

19 oz. (540 mL) cans of white kidney beans, rinsed and drained	2	2
14 oz. (398 mL) cans of stewed tomatoes, cut up	2	2
Prepared vegetable broth	1 cup	250 mL
Chili powder	1 tsp.	5 mL
Paprika	1/2 tsp.	2 mL
Garlic powder	1/2 tsp.	2 mL
Onion powder	1/2 tsp.	2 mL
Crushed red pepper flakes	1/2 tsp.	2 mL
No-salt seasoning	1/4 tsp.	1 mL
Frozen mixed vegetables, thawed	3 cups	750 mL

Combine first 4 ingredients in a 3 1/2 to 4 quart (3.5 to 4 L) slow cooker. Cook, covered, on Low for 6 to 8 hours, or on High for 3 to 4 hours.

Stir in vegetables. Cook, covered, on High for about 30 minutes until vegetables are tender. Serves 4.

1 serving: 320 Calories; 0.5 g Total Fat (0 g Mono, 0 g Poly, 0 g Sat); 0 mg Cholesterol; 60 g Carbohydrate (22 g Fibre, 16 g Sugar); 17 g Protein; 850 mg Sodium

African Sweet Potato Stew

Primarily sweet with the flavours of peanut butter and sweet potato, this stew also has a bit of cayenne heat. It can be served on its own or with brown rice, and can be frozen in an airtight container for up to three months.

Chopped peeled orange-fleshed sweet potato (1 inch, 2.5 cm, pieces)	5 cups	1.25 L
Halved fresh white mushrooms	2 cups	500 mL
Chopped fresh pineapple	1 1/2 cups	375 mL
Dried green lentils	3/4 cup	175 mL
Canola oil	2 tsp.	10 mL
Chopped onion	1 1/2 cups	375 mL
Tomato paste (see Tip, page 18)	2 tbsp.	30 mL
Curry powder	2 tsp.	10 mL
Finely grated ginger root (or 1/4 tsp., 1 mL, ground ginger)	1 tsp.	5 mL
Cayenne pepper	1/4 tsp.	1 mL
Garlic clove, minced (or 1/4 tsp., 1 mL, powder)	1	1
Prepared low-sodium vegetable broth	2 cups	500 mL
Beer	1 cup	500 mL
Chopped fresh spinach leaves, lightly packed	1 cup	250 mL
Peanut butter	1/2 cup	125 mL
Lime juice	2 tbsp.	30 mL

Place first 4 ingredients in a greased 4 to 5 quart (4 to 5 L) slow cooker.

Heat canola oil in a large frying pan on medium. Add onion. Cook for about 5 minutes, stirring often, until softened.

Add next 5 ingredients. Heat, stirring, for about 1 minute until fragrant.

Add first amount of broth and beer. Heat, stirring carefully, until boiling. Transfer to slow cooker. Stir. Cook, covered, on Low for 6 to 7 hours, or on High for 3 to 3 1/2 hours.

Add remaining 3 ingredients. Stir well. Serves 6.

1 serving: 380 Calories; 13 g Total Fat (1 g Mono, 0.5 g Poly, 2 g Sat); 0 mg Cholesterol; 52 g Carbohydrate (10 g Fibre, 13 g Sugar); 15 g Protein; 95 mg Sodium

Lasagna Fagiole

Romano beans give this lasagna a smooth and creamy texture, and the short list of ingredients makes it so easy to assemble.

Cooking oil	2 tsp.	10 mL
Chopped onion	2 cups	250 mL
Mushrooms, sliced	2 cups	500 mL
Pepper	1/4 tsp.	1 mL
Tomato garlic pasta sauce	3 1/2 cups	875 mL
19 oz. (540 mL) can of romano beans, rinsed and drained	1	1
Water	1 cup	250 mL
10 oz. (300 g) boxes of frozen spinach, thawed, drained and chopped	2	2
Low-fat ricotta cheese	2/3 cup	150 mL
Oven-ready lasagna noodles, broken in half	9	9
Grated mozzarella cheese	2 cups	500 mL

Heat cooking oil in a large frying pan on medium. Add onion and mushrooms. Sprinkle with pepper. Cook for about 10 minutes, stirring often, until onion is softened and water from mushrooms is evaporated.

Stir in next 3 ingredients. Remove from heat.

Combine spinach and ricotta in a medium bowl.

Layer ingredients in greased 5 to 7 quart (5 to 7 L) slow cooker as follows:

1. 1/4 bean mixture

2. 6 noodle halves

3. 1/4 bean mixture

4. 1/2 the spinach mixture

5. 1 cup (250 mL) cheese

6. 6 noodle halves

7. 1/4 bean mixture

8. Remaining spinach mixture

9. Remaining noodle halves

10. Remaining bean mixture

11. Remaining cheese

Cook, covered, on Low for 4 to 5 hours, or on High for 2 to 2 1/2 hours. Let stand, uncovered, for 10 minutes. Serves 6.

1 serving: 320 Calories; 11 g Total Fat (1.5 g Mono, 0.5 g Poly, 5 g Sat); 30 mg Cholesterol; 40 g Carbohydrate (10 g Fibre, 10 g Sugar); 19 g Protein; 850 mg Sodium

Caribbean Vegetable Rice

Coconut rice and tender vegetables with flavours reminiscent of jerk seasoning.
Pumpkin seeds add an interesting final touch.

Chopped peeled orange-fleshed sweet potato (about 3/4 inch, 2 cm, pieces)	4 cups	1 L
Chopped cauliflower	3 cups	750 mL
Chopped yellow pepper (3/4 inch, 2 cm, pieces)	2 cups	500 mL
Chopped onion	1 cup	250 mL
Long-grain brown rice	1 cup	250 mL
14 oz. (398 mL) can of coconut milk	1	1
Prepared vegetable broth	1 cup	250 mL
Brown sugar, packed	1 tbsp.	15 mL
Chili paste (sambal oelek)	1 tbsp.	15 mL
Finely grated ginger root (or 1/2 tsp., 2 mL, ground ginger)	2 tsp.	10 mL
Garlic cloves, minced (or 1/2 tsp., 2 mL, powder)	2	2
Dried thyme	1/2 tsp.	2 mL
Ground allspice	1/2 tsp.	2 mL
Ground cinnamon	1/4 tsp.	1 mL
Salt	1/2 tsp.	2 mL
Pepper	1/4 tsp.	1 mL
Chopped unsalted toasted pumpkin seeds	1/3 cup	75 mL

Combine first 5 ingredients in a greased 3 1/2 to 4 quart (3.5 to 4 L) slow cooker.

Whisk next 11 ingredients in a medium bowl. Stir into vegetables in slow cooker. Cook, covered, on Low for 8 to 9 hours, or on High for 4 to 4 1/2 hours.

Sprinkle with pumpkin seeds. Serves 6.

1 serving: 390 Calories; 16 g Total Fat (1 g Mono, 0.5 g Poly, 13 g Sat); 0 mg Cholesterol; 57 g Carbohydrate (7 g Fibre, 9 g Sugar); 7 g Protein; 420 mg Sodium

Megadarra

In this classic Lebanese dish, the sweetness of the onions and the earthiness of the lentils are a delicious combination. You can use any colour lentil, but adjust the cooking time accordingly. Serve with a crisp green salad.

Olive (or cooking) oil	1 tbsp.	15 mL
Thinly sliced onion	3 1/2 cups	875 mL
Brown sugar, packed	2 tbsp.	30 mL
Red wine vinegar	1 tbsp.	15 mL
Dried green lentils, rinsed	1 cup	250 mL
Prepared low-sodium vegetable broth	3 cups	750 mL
Water	1 cup	250 mL
Coarse ground pepper	1/2 tsp.	2 mL
Ground allspice	1/2 tsp.	2 mL
Ground coriander	1/2 tsp.	2 mL
Brown converted rice	1/2 cup	125 mL
Chopped fresh parsley (or 1 1/2 tsp., 7 mL, flakes)	2 tbsp.	30 mL

Heat olive oil in a large frying pan on medium. Add onion. Cook for about 20 minutes, stirring often, until caramelized.

Add brown sugar and vinegar. Heat, stirring, for 1 minute. Remove from heat. Put into a 3 1/2 to 4 quart (3.5 to 4 L) slow cooker

Stir in next 7 ingredients. Cook, covered, on Low for about 7 to 8 hours, or on High for 3 1/2 to 4 hours.

Stir in parsley. Serves 5.

1 serving: 350 Calories; 5 g Total Fat (2.5 g Mono, 0 g Poly, 0.5 g Sat); 0 mg Cholesterol; 65 g Carbohydrate (10 g Fibre, 13 g Sugar); 15 g Protein; 510 mg Sodium

Rice Lentil Casserole

This convenient one-dish meal of lentils, rice, tomatoes and mozzarella has deliciously satisfying flavour and texture.

Prepared low-sodium vegetable broth	2 1/2 cups	625 mL
14 oz. (398 mL) can of diced tomatoes (with juice)	1	1
Chopped onion	1 cup	250 mL
Diced carrot	1 cup	250 mL
Dried green lentils	3/4 cup	175 mL
Grated mozzarella cheese	3/4 cup	175 mL
Long-grain brown rice	3/4 cup	175 mL
4 oz. (113 g) can of diced green chilies	1	1
Dried basil	1/2 tsp.	2 mL
Dried oregano	1/2 tsp.	2 mL
Garlic cloves, minced (or 1/2 tsp., 2 mL, powder)	2	2
Salt	1/4 tsp.	1 mL
Fresh oregano, chopped	2 tbsp.	30 mL

Combine first 12 ingredients in a 4 quart (4 L) slow cooker. Cook, covered, on Low for 7 to 8 hours, or on High for 3 1/2 to 4 hours.

Stir in oregano. Serves 4.

1 serving: 350 Calories; 4.5 g Total Fat (0 g Mono, 0 g Poly, 2 g Sat); 10 mg Cholesterol; 64 g Carbohydrate (17 g Fibre, 7 g Sugar); 17 g Protein; 680 mg Sodium

Chickpea Pasta Casserole

An appetizing dish with hearty chickpeas, tangy tomatoes and creamy goat cheese. Any bite-sized pasta may be used in place of ditali, but refer to the package directions for varied cook times.

Water	8 cups	2 L
Salt	1 tsp.	5 mL
Ditali pasta	1 1/2 cups	375 mL
Chopped cauliflower	1 cup	250 mL
Chopped carrots	1/2 cup	125 mL
Chopped celery	1/2 cup	125 mL
28 oz. (796 mL) can of diced tomatoes (with juice) rinsed and drained	1	1
Chopped zucchini (with peel)	1 cup	250 mL
Finely chopped onion	1/2 cup	125 mL
Goat (chèvre) cheese, cut up	4 oz.	113 g
Sun-dried tomato pesto	2 tbsp.	30 mL
Red wine vinegar	1 tbsp.	15 mL
Garlic cloves, minced (or 1/2 tsp., 2 mL, powder)	2	2
Dried basil	1 tsp.	5 mL
Crushed dried rosemary	1/2 tsp	2 mL
Granulated sugar	1/2 tsp.	2 mL
Crushed unseasoned croutons	1/2 cup	125 mL
Butter (or hard margarine), melted	1 tbsp.	15 mL
Chopped fresh basil	1 tbsp.	15 mL

Bring water and salt to boil in a Dutch oven. Add pasta and cook, uncovered, for 5 minutes, stirring occasionally. Drain and transfer to a 4 to 5 quart (4 to 5 L) slow cooker.

Stir in next 13 ingredients. Cook, covered, on Low for 6 to 7 hours, or on High for 3 to 3 1/2 hours.

Combine croutons, butter and basil in a small bowl. Sprinkle over pasta mixture. Cook on High for 15 minutes. Serves 8.

1 serving: 250 Calories; 7 g Total Fat (1 g Mono, 0 g Poly, 3.5 g Sat); 36 mg Cholesterol; 7 g Carbohydrate (7 g Fibre, 5 g Sugar); 12 g Protein; 260 mg Sodium

Tofu Vegetable Curry

Serve this colourful, aromatic blend of veggies and browned tofu with brown rice or whole wheat naan. Garnish with sliced hot pepper for more heat.

12 1/2 oz. (350 g) package of firm tofu, cut into 3/4 inch (2 cm) cubes	1	1
Mild curry paste	1 tsp.	5 mL
Canola oil	2 tsp.	10 mL
Canola oil	2 tsp.	10 mL
Sliced onion	2 cups	500 mL
Mild curry paste	1 tbsp.	15 mL
Garlic cloves, minced	2	2
Prepared vegetable broth	2 cups	500 mL
Cauliflower or broccoli florets	2 cups	500 mL
Cubed butternut squash, cut into 1 inch (2.5 cm) pieces	2 cups	500 mL
Cubed eggplant, cut into 1 inch (2.5 cm) pieces	1 cup	250 mL
Sliced orange pepper	1 cup	250 mL
Sliced mushrooms	1/2 cup	125 mL
Water	1 tbsp.	15 mL
Cornstarch	1 tsp.	5 mL
Chopped fresh spinach leaves, lightly packed	1 1/2 cups	375 mL
Frozen peas	1 cup	250 mL
Chopped tomato	1 cup	250 mL
Brown sugar, packed	2 tsp.	10 mL

Toss tofu and first amount of curry paste in a medium bowl. Heat first amount of canola oil in a large frying pan on medium-high. Add tofu. Cook for about 8 minutes, stirring occasionally, until browned. Transfer to a large plate. Cool. Chill, covered.

Heat second amount of canola oil in same frying pan on medium. Add onion. Cook for about 8 minutes, stirring often, until softened. Add second amount of curry paste and garlic. Heat, stirring, for about 1 minute until fragrant. Add broth. Heat, stirring and scraping any brown bits from bottom of pan, until boiling. Transfer to 4 to 5 quart (4 to 5 L) slow cooker.

Stir in next 5 ingredients. Cook, covered, on Low for 4 to 5 hours, or on High for 2 to 2 1/2 hours.

Stir water into cornstarch in a small cup until smooth. Add to slow cooker. Stir in remaining 4 ingredients and tofu. Cook, covered, on High for about 15 minutes until boiling and thickened. Serves 6.

1 serving: *200 Calories; 8 g Total Fat (2 g Mono, 1 g Poly, 1 g Sat); 0 mg Cholesterol; 22 g Carbohydrate (4 g Fibre, 7 g Sugar); 11 g Protein; 290 mg Sodium*

Moroccan Veggie Casserole

This dish will fill your kitchen with the scents of Morocco and whisk you on a culinary journey to the streets of Marrakesh.

Chopped peeled orange-fleshed sweet potato	2 cups	500 mL
Prepared vegetable broth	2 cups	500 mL
Chopped onion	1 cup	250 mL
Chopped red pepper	1 cup	250 mL
Chopped zucchini (with peel), cut into 1/2 inch (12 mm) pieces	1 cup	250 mL
Long-grain brown rice	1 cup	250 mL
Dry (or alcohol-free) white wine	3/4 cup	175 mL
Dried apricots, chopped	1/2 cup	125 mL
Raisins	1/2 cup	125 mL
Chopped tomato	1/2 cup	125 mL
Lemon juice	2 tbsp.	30 mL
Liquid honey	2 tsp.	10 mL
Ground cinnamon	1/4 tsp.	1 mL
Ground cumin	1/4 tsp.	1 mL
Ground ginger	1/4 tsp.	1 mL

Combine all 15 ingredients in a 3 to 4 quart (3 to 4 L) slow cooker. Cook, covered, on Low for 6 to 7 hours, or on High for 3 to 3 1/2 hours. Serves 5.

1 serving: 340 Calories; 1.5 g Total Fat (0 g Mono, 0 g Poly, 0 g Sat); 0 mg Cholesterol; 74 g Carbohydrate (7 g Fibre, 27 g Sugar); 5 g Protein; 270 mg Sodium

Vegetarian Chipotle Chili

On a cold, blustery day, nothing hits the spot like a bowl of homemade chili. The chipotle peppers add a mild, smokey heat.

28 oz. (796 mL) can of diced tomatoes with juice	1	1
19 oz. (540 mL) can of red kidney beans, rinsed and drained	1	1
15 oz. (425 mL) can of great northern beans, rinsed and drained	1	1
White mushrooms, thickly sliced	2 cups	500 mL
Celery, chopped	1 1/2 cups	375 mL
Red pepper, chopped	1 1/2 cups	375 mL
Onion, chopped	1 1/2 cups	375 mL
Zucchini, coarsely chopped	1 1/2 cups	375 mL
Tomato paste (see Tip, page 18)	3 tbsp.	45 mL
Chili powder	2 tbsp.	30 mL
Chopped chipotle peppers in adobo sauce (see Tip, page 44)	2 tsp.	10 mL
Ground cumin	1 tsp.	5 mL
Sugar	1/2 tsp.	2 mL
Salt	1/4 tsp.	1 mL

Combine all 14 ingredients in a 4 to 5 quart (4 to 5 L) slow cooker. Cook, covered, on Low for 8 to 9 hours, or on High for 4 to 4 1/2 hours. Serves 6.

1 serving: 230 Calories; 2.5 g Total Fat (0 g Mono, 0 g Poly, 0 g Sat); 0 mg Cholesterol; 44 g Carbohydrate (15 g Fibre, 9 g Sugar); 14 g Protein; 330 mg Sodium

Mexican Quinoa

A delicious, light, healthy meal that is perfect for a fiesta but easy enough to prepare for dinner on a busy weeknight. Quinoa can be used as a great alternative for rice in many Mexican dishes.

Cubed acorn squash	4 cups	1 L
Frozen kernel corn	1 cup	250 mL
19 oz. (540 mL) can of pinto beans, rinsed and drained	1	1
Garlic cloves, crushed	2	2
Quinoa, rinsed	1 cup	250 mL
14 oz. (398 mL) can of low-sodium diced tomatoes (with juice)	1	1
19 oz. (540 mL) cans of tomato sauce	2	2
Prepared vegetable broth	3/4 cup	175 mL
Lime juice	1/4 cup	60 mL
Chopped chipotle pepper in adobo sauce (see Tip, page 44)	1 tbsp.	15 mL
Ground cumin	1 tsp.	5 mL
Dried oregano	1 tsp.	5 mL
Spicy no-salt seasoning	1 tsp.	5 mL
Chili powder	1/2 tsp.	5 mL
Pepper	1/2 tsp.	5 mL
Chopped zucchini	1 cup	250 mL
Chopped cilantro	3 tbsp.	45 mL
Lime wedges	6	6

Combine first 9 ingredients in a 4 to 5 quart (4 to 5 L) slow cooker.

Combine next 6 ingredients in a small bowl. Stir into quinoa mixture. Cook, covered, on Low for 6 to 7 hours, or on High for 3 to 4 hours.

Stir in zucchini and cook, covered, on High for 15 minutes. Sprinkle with cilantro, and serve with lime wedges. Serves 6.

1 serving: 300 Calories; 5 g Total Fat (0 g Mono, 0 g Poly, 0.5 g Sat); 0 mg Cholesterol; 63 g Carbohydrate (13 g Fibre, 4 g Sugar); 13 g Protein; 430 mg Sodium

INDEX